Researching Serendipity in Digital Information Environments

Synthesis Lectures on Information Concepts, Retrieval, and Services

Editor

Gary Marchionini, *University of North Carolina, Chapel Hill*

Synthesis Lectures on Information Concepts, Retrieval, and Services publishes short books on topics pertaining to information science and applications of technology to information discovery, production, distribution, and management. Potential topics include: data models, indexing theory and algorithms, classification, information architecture, information economics, privacy and identity, scholarly communication, bibliometrics and webometrics, personal information management, human information behavior, digital libraries, archives and preservation, cultural informatics, information retrieval evaluation, data fusion, relevance feedback, recommendation systems, question answering, natural language processing for retrieval, text summarization, multimedia retrieval, multilingual retrieval, and exploratory search.

Researching Serendipity in Digital Information Environments
Lori McCay-Peet and Elaine G. Toms

ISBN: 978-3-031-01184-9 print
ISBN: 978-3-031-02312-5 ebook

DOI: 10.1007/978-3-031-02312-5

A Publication in the Springer series
SYNTHESIS LECTURES ON INFORMATION CONCEPTS, RETRIEVAL, AND SERVICES, #59
Series Editor: Gary Marchionini, University of North Carolina, Chapel Hill

Series ISSN: 1947-945X Print   1947-9468 Electronic

Researching Serendipity in Digital Information Environments

Lori McCay-Peet
Dalhousie University

Elaine G. Toms
The University of Sheffield

SYNTHESIS LECTURES ON INFORMATION CONCEPTS, RETRIEVAL, AND SERVICES #59

ABSTRACT

Chance, luck, and good fortune are the usual go-to descriptors of serendipity, a phenomenon aptly often coupled with famous anecdotes of accidental discoveries in engineering and science in modern history such as penicillin, Teflon, and Post-it notes. Serendipity, however, is evident in many fields of research, in organizations, in everyday life—and there is more to it than luck implies. While the phenomenon is strongly associated with in-person interactions with people, places, and things, most attention of late has focused on its preservation and facilitation within digital information environments. Serendipity's association with unexpected, positive user experiences and outcomes has spurred an interest in understanding both how current digital information environments support serendipity and how novel approaches may be developed to facilitate it. Research has sought to understand serendipity, how it is manifested in people's personality traits and behaviors, how it may be facilitated in digital information environments such as mobile applications, and its impacts on an individual, an organizational, and a wider level. Because serendipity is expressed and understood in different ways in different contexts, multiple methods have been used to study the phenomenon and evaluate digital information environments that may support it. This volume brings together different disciplinary perspectives and examines the motivations for studying serendipity, the various ways in which serendipity has been approached in the research, methodological approaches to build theory, and how it may be facilitated. Finally, a roadmap for serendipity research is drawn by integrating key points from this volume to produce a framework for the examination of serendipity in digital information environments.

KEYWORDS

serendipity, digital information environments, user experience, human–centered information retrieval, human–computer interaction

Contents

Preface

Serendipity...the word conjures up an image of that fortuitous finding, one that evokes a happy human response. From its unassuming roots in literary scholarship in the Georgian era, the concept emerged in the 20th century to represent fortuitous discoveries perceived to be by chance, but clearly informed by significant knowledge and experience. Often equated with scientific discoveries it has evolved to be now associated with that unexpected but informed outcome in the social sciences and humanities and indeed in everyday life.

When we think of serendipity in digital information environments, we are constrained by physicality of that setting—the digital device, and also by the range of activities that may occur within that space and contexts. This book starts with an understanding of its initial origins and application and transfers that understanding to its application to and evolution in digital spaces. It examines the motivation for a renewed and intense interest in serendipity in research and development (R&D), and identifies the various interpretations of serendipity (e.g., event, outcome, process) that have been made to inform a better understanding of where and how to approach the concept in R&D. It examines how we can and do facilitate serendipity in digital spaces, and how, methodologically, to research the concept in these spaces.

To start such a work, we put our assumptions and perspectives about serendipity aside, and began with a "clean slate." We conducted a systematic review of the research on serendipity, first searching broadly in four databases (Web of Science, ProQuest, EBSCO, and ACM Digital Library) for papers that serve as the basis for Chapters 2–5. In May 2016, we downloaded 1,293 citations but after removing duplicates and doing an initial cull based on title and abstract to ensure topic fit, we selected 550 for a closer look. From these, as well as papers subsequently gathered through other methods (e.g., citation chaining), we selected approximately 100 papers that met the following conditions for a more thorough examination.

- Paper was a published, peer-reviewed study of serendipity in digital environments; literature reviews, conceptual papers, and theses were not considered in the systematic review.

- Papers that mentioned serendipity only superficially were not considered.

- No restrictions on how authors defined serendipity.

- Research was empirical, using either or both qualitative or quantitative methods, but with no restrictions on method or methodology.

- No restrictions on research area or topic with respect to:

  ○ information use environment (e.g., work leisure, learning, commerce);

  ○ domain, field, or area (e.g., science, history, education);

  ○ platform, application, or service (e.g., Twitter, WorldCat);

  ○ type of digital device (e.g., mobile, laptop, wearable); and

  ○ content or its format (e.g., text, image, sound).

Seminal works that do not meet the above criteria (e.g., Merton and Barber, 2004) are also referenced throughout the volume, but by conducting the systematic review, we hope that we have provided a useful "state-of-the-art" synthesis of the research on serendipity in digital information environments.

Lori McCay-Peet and Elaine G. Toms
July 2017

Acknowledgments

We are grateful to many colleagues, whose insights and exchanges have contributed over the years to our thinking about serendipity, including Lennart Björneborn, Samantha Copeland, Sanda Erdelez, Jannica Heinström, Stephann Makri, Kim Martin, Anabel Quan-Haase, and Borchuluun Yadamsuren. A SSHRC Aid to Workshops and Conferences Program grant enabled *SCORE: Serendipity, Chance and Opportunity in Information Discovery*, a workshop hosted in Montreal in 2012, to bring together a group of researchers to unpeel the concept of serendipity in digital information environments.

We also acknowledge financial support for the research that informed much of the thinking behind this volume. Toms' initial research on browsing in digital user environments (which serendipitously introduced her research to serendipity) was funded by a NSERC (Natural Sciences and Engineering Research Council of Canada) grant to her Ph.D. supervisor, Professor Jean Tague-Sutcliffe, University of Western Ontario (now Western University). Their individual and joint research, including McCay-Peet's Ph.D. work, was partially funded by a SSHRC (Social Sciences and Humanities Research Council of Canada) Research Grant, on *Serendipity in Knowledge Work* to Toms; and a SSHRC Doctoral Scholarship to McCay-Peet. Finally, we acknowledge the support of the Canada Foundation for Innovation that funded the research infrastructure that enabled multiple research projects, and Dalhousie University, Halifax, Nova Scotia, Canada who hosted the research projects.

CHAPTER 1

Introduction

Mention serendipity to anyone anywhere and it congers up an immediate pleasurable reaction. Many have stories to tell about serendipitous moments when something materialized—an idea or opportunity—often from an interaction with an object or person in the immediate environment. Sometimes it appeared, as though by magic, as a lightning-bolt, thought-in-head. But, whatever *it* was, it was perceived as value-added, and not previously contemplated or considered.

When we think of serendipity, we associate it first with scientific discoveries and inventions such as dynamite, rubber, penicillin, microwave, photography, X-rays, radioactivity, Liquorice All-sorts, Post-it notes, Viagra, laughing gas, Velcro, Teflon, and Nylon. Arguably, Columbus' discovery of North America occurred when he was looking for a new trade route to the Orient—a serendipitous find. In this book, we start from those early explanations and understanding of serendipity and consider the concept in the context of digital information environments.

But when is something truly serendipitous? Serendipity is often associated with chance, blind luck, fortuitous events, and accidental coincidences, but these words are not synonymous with serendipity, as many authors have lamented (see, for example, De Rond, 2014; Merton and Barber, 2004; Shaprio, 1986). As you will discover on reading this book, for an event, process, outcome, or experience to be serendipitous, it needs several conditions.

- A person is exposed to an object that is unusual, but is *meaningfully* unusual.

- The person has the sagacity to observe, identify, and extract elements from the object, and the mental space and tenacity to re-use them in a new way.

- The outcome is unanticipated such that under normal circumstances it would not be predicted.

In short, we are looking at "planned insight coupled with unplanned events" (Fine and Deegan, 1996, p. 435). There is an element of surprise and chance, but an element that can only be acted on by someone capable of understanding, extracting and using that chance finding.

Serendipity may have global impact such as the discoveries and inventions mentioned earlier. But equally it may be very individual such that the chance discovery enabled a similarly unexpected (to the person) find that may not have consequences beyond that person's sphere.

In this chapter, we examine the concept of serendipity, its historic roots, its problematic nomenclature, and how something that is characterized as serendipitous unfolds.

1.1   ORIGINS OF SERENDIPITY

Serendipity has its roots in the 18th century, but was not popularly used until the second half of the 20th century. Today a search of Google will net over 30 million occurrences, and Google Scholar outputs over 100,000 occurrences in the scholarly literature. This is in contrast with Merton and Barber (2004) who identified only 135 people from the word's origin to the mid-20th century who had used the word in print. Remarkably, there is no equivalent word in some languages (Martinez, 2011).

The first use of the word, serendipity, appeared in a letter dated January 28, 1754 from a man of letters and politician, Horace Walpole, known for his neologisms, to his friend and diplomat, Horace Mann. In that letter, Walpole was commenting on his search for an image about a Venetian coat of arms. He writes:

> This discovery indeed is almost of that kind which I call serendipity, a very expressive word, which as I have nothing better to tell you, I shall endeavour to explain to you: you will understand it better by the derivation than by definition. I once read a silly fairy tale, called The Three Princes of Serendip: as their Highnesses travelled, they were always making discoveries, by accidents and sagacity, of things which they were not in quest of: for instance, one of them discovered that a mule blind in the right eye had travelled the same road lately, because the grass was eaten only on the left side, where it was worse than on right—now do you understand serendipity? One of the most remarkable instances of this accidental sagacity (for you must observe that no discovery of a thing you are looking for comes under this description) was of my Lord Shaftsbury, who happening to dine at Lord Chancellor Clarendon's, found out the marriage of the Duke of York and Mrs. Hyde, by the respect which her mother treated her at the table (as quoted in Remer, 1965, p. 6).

The key point of the story is that three odd observations led the princes to identify the characteristics of a mule even though they had neither seen the mule, nor were looking for a mule. It was a case of insightful observation and inference (Merton and Barber, 2004). Similarly, in the second also unusual example over dinner, shrewd observation coupled with sagacity led to an unexpected conclusion (and one would need to be an expert in the etiquette of the day to fully grasp the logic). Walpole's seemingly innocuous reflections informed the concept of serendipity that we still use to this day, a concept that intertwines acute mental discernment and accident to explain a discovery.

Walpole's concept remained a private communiqué between the two friends, until Walpole's correspondence was published in the 1830s. It took another 40 years before the word resurfaced in a public medium. In 1875, it appeared in formal print in the English language in the journal *Notes and Queries*, where Edward Solly introduced it into literary groups (Merton and Barber, 2004). Even though many incidences of serendipitous findings occurred in science during this period (e.g., vulcanization of rubber, coal tar dye mauve), the word, serendipity, was not used to describe them.

In 1909, serendipity had its first appearance in a dictionary, *The Century Dictionary and Cyclopedia*, (the precursor to the *Encyclopedia Britannica*) and in 1913 it appeared in the *Oxford English Dictionary*. From the early 1900s to about 1935, serendipity remained used almost exclusively by literary scholars. In the mid-1930s, scientists and, in particular, Cannon (1945) at the Harvard Medical School popularized its role in scientific discovery (Merton and Barber, 2004). The pendulum swung from a dominant use in describing discoveries in science, although serendipity is now widely used throughout all disciplines.

In 1958, Merton and Barber wrote a detailed account of serendipity, but the book languished as a manuscript until 2004 when it was published shortly before Merton's death. This work, however, remains the most comprehensive discussion of the concept. Since that time, Walpole's "very expressive word" has entered everyday conversation to describe everything from surprises to random occurrences and unexplained but happy outcomes (Merton and Barber, 2004, p. 4). But we believe that the common use in everyday language has led to dilution in its meaning, which challenges its application in research.

1.2   ON DEFINING SERENDIPITY

Part of the confusion over what is meant by serendipity can be attributed to Walpole (Remer, 1965; Merton and Barber, 2004) who did not make clear how the concept was to be defined and thus used. Merton and Barber (2004) examined its appearance in dictionaries from its conception to the end of the 20th century and concluded that it had been perceived as an "esoteric word" given that it did not appear in any of the abridged dictionaries until 1951.

How it appears in dictionaries illustrates its lack of specificity as these examples demonstrate.

1. An aptitude for making desirable discoveries by accident; good fortune; luck ("serendipity," n.d.-a).

2. The faculty of making fortunate discoveries by accident; the fact or occurrence of such discoveries; an instance of making such a discovery ("serendipity," n.d.-b).

3. The faculty or phenomenon of finding valuable or agreeable things not sought for ("serendipity," n.d.-c).

4. The occurrence and development of events by chance in a happy or beneficial way ("serendipity," n.d.-d).

5. The faculty of finding valuable or interesting things by chance or where one least expects them ("serendipity," 1932).

The challenge with these definitions is their use primarily of adjectives (e.g., desirable, fortunate, valuable, agreeable, happy, interesting) that are difficult to operationalize. While the use of the words faculty and aptitude in the definitions suggest ability on the part of the individual experiencing serendipity, sagacity and the prepared mind are missing, suggesting that to be serendipitous is, largely, to be lucky. From a research perspective, we need to deconstruct and operationalize the terminology so that we recognize the phenomena that we are investigating. For greater clarity, we look instead to how serendipity is deployed by those who research it.

For an incident to be described as serendipitous, or for an outcome to claim to be serendipity, it will have the following five conditions:

1. There is an observation that is unanticipated, anomalous, unexpected, unpredictable, or inconsistent with existing findings or theories. This is a core condition and is generally agreed on by all who have researched serendipity (see, for example, Danzico, 2010; Foster and Ford, 2003; Makri and Blandford, 2012; McCay-Peet and Toms, 2015; Merton and Barber, 2004; Toms, 1997). But it is not the only characteristic. Many discussions of serendipity stop here, but in doing so interpret serendipity as simply synonymous with surprises and apparently happy random accidents; "without an element of chance, 'discovery' is nothing more than verification; without sagacity, it is mere happenstance" (Arvo, 1999, p. 183).

2. The individual involved must have the human cognitive capacity and ability or knowledge and experience to make that observation—the prepared mind—which is often an observation that many have failed to notice, recognize, or even consider. From penicillin to dynamite, and microwave ovens to Post-it notes and Velcro, the "know-how" of the person making the observation is integral to the discovery. Chemist Paul Flory, on receiving the 1977 Perkin Medal, noted,

Significant inventions are not mere accidents. The erroneous view [that they are] is widely held, and it is one that the scientific and technical community, unfortunately, has done little to dispel. Happenstance usually plays a part, to be sure, but there is much more to invention than the popular notion of a bolt out of the blue. Knowledge in depth and in breadth are virtual prerequisites. Unless the mind is thoroughly charged beforehand, the proverbial spark of genius, if it should manifest itself, probably will find nothing to ignite (Flory, 1977, p. 4).

Similarly, medieval historian, Julian Luxford (2009) was researching two topics at once (sources for his book on medieval drawings and decoration in Carthusiasn manuscripts) when he stumbled upon a rare negative reference to Robin Hood in the marginalia of a 13th century medieval manuscript in the Eton school library. Even though other medieval scholars had examined the same manuscript, only he both recognized the find, and went on to write about the out-of-the-ordinary discovery. His knowledge of the era and context enabled him to recognize the value of the scribble.

Pasteur astutely reached the same conclusion illustrated above a century earlier; it is not about luck and chance, but also about knowledge and experience. In a 1854 speech to the Faculté des Sciences at Lille, Pasteur made his now famous quote in describing the discovery of the technology underlying the telegraph. As he relayed it, Orsted observed the movement of a magnetic needle "suddenly by chance, you might say, but remember, that in the sciences of observation, chance favors the mind which is prepared." [1]

In all of these cases there was an "intellectual preparedness" (Fine and Deegan, 1996) that enabled the researcher to understand the value of the observation, and then to allow for the "ah ha" moment to occur. If a person only sees what one is looking for, then one may miss the chance discovery.

3. While the individual needs the ability based on knowledge and experience to sense the anomaly and its import, the individual also must have the human mental space at that time to absorb it, and recognize its value, and the perseverance to then act on it. Fleming (1964) in his 1945 Nobel speech described his discovery:

> ...I prefer to tell the truth, that penicillin started as a chance observation. My only merit is that I did not neglect the observation and that I pursued the subject as a bacteriologist (p. 83).

It takes a person in the right "mental space" to observe, interpret and seize the opportunity.

Surprises and accidents and incidental information encountering occur every day to everyone. But not everyone can turn that surprise or accident or new piece of information into a significant outcome. From the examples mentioned earlier, how many other people were exposed to the same or similar set of circumstances but failed to see the relevance? "The "natural tendency of the unprepared mind is to discard the unusual" (Rosenau as quoted in Merton and Barber, 2004, p. 179).

Perhaps the most fitting example is the case of the floppy rabbit ears (Barber and Fox, 1958). Two eminent medical research groups separately and nearly simultaneously noticed that the normally stiff upright ears of rabbits flopped when the rabbits were injected with a particular enzyme. Both considered it abnormal and anomalous, and initially put the observation aside. Five years later, one of the researchers, Lewis Thomas, followed up on his curiosity noting that the enzyme also attacked the cartilage in bones and joints and led him to connect the observation to his interest in

---

[1] This is the English translation of the comment made in French: "a Dans les champs de l'observation le hazard ne favorise que les esprits préparés."

human disease and its relevance to rheumatoid arthritis and emphysema (Bashyam, 2007). One researcher followed up on the observation, while the other ignored it. Both were equally capable and had the knowledge to pursue it.

4. Incubation, consumption, and follow-up time is a factor in all phenomena described as serendipitous, and it is this factor which exacerbates our ability to research serendipity. While we often delight in Archimedes "Eureka!" it is a rarity that an observation is made and a discovery is realized in the blink of an eye. There is a gestation period so that the anomaly or surprise can be explored, interpreted, and analyzed, as the case of the floppy ears attests; this aspect is typically attributed to the creative process (Herrmann, 1989). Pasteur was purported to have said "Let me tell you the secret that has led to my goal: my strength lies solely in my tenacity."

5. There is a valuable outcome. In the sciences, it may have global ramifications such as the discovery of penicillin, radioactivity and smart dust. But at the individual level, it may lead to a change in direction, or personal problem solved. It is in the outcome that the relationship between serendipity and creativity become apparent: "creativity involves coming up with something novel, something different. And, in order to be interesting, it must be something intelligible and must relate to that which we know before" (Boden, 1996, p. 165), but it most likely will be something that no one has thought of before (Shaprio, 1986). However, serendipity is not a mirror image of the creative process; serendipity is a divergent process that may also discover a problem (Campos and de Figueiredo, 2002) that does not fit the usual creative process.

In summary, for an event, outcome or process to be serendipitous, it is initiated with an anomalous observation by a person who has the requisite skills to observe its irregularity, and the mental space to follow through on the observation, taking whatever requisite time is required to turn it into an unexpected finding. This is a time-tested process well documented in the physical world in science, medicine and technology in particular. This now serves as a basis for our examination of serendipity in digital information environments. Table 3.1 illustrates how five research groups who have studied serendipity in digital information environments have conceptualized the elements of serendipity primarily as a linear process, but influenced by additional elements. Chapter 4 shows how we have adapted the physical world perspective described above to the digital information environment.

1.3   HOW SERENDIPITY HAPPENS

From the origins and use of the concept to date, three potential interpretations of how serendipity unfolds have emerged. They serve as a useful approach in understanding and deconstructing the process. Rather than enter that debate (e.g., is pseudo serendipity really serendipity?), we instead associate all three with serendipity although each has its supporters and naysayers. The three types are described below and illustrated in Figure 1.1. Examples are provided for each, all drawn from the sciences because they provide concrete illustrations of the three ways serendipity has been described to date. These types will be further explored specifically in relation to digital information environments in Chapter 4.

- Type A. *From Observations to Solution*

  An individual makes an observation that leads to the discovery of something novel; neither the observation nor the outcome is the objective of the investigation. This was the basis on which Walpole created the concept. In his description of the tale, the three princes were not looking for anything; they were able to solve a problem once they were presented with the clues. This has been described as abduction—"a form of reasoning to discover something new" (as discussed in Van Andel, 1994, p. 636), but regardless of the reasoning process, Type A meets the five conditions discussed in Section 1.2.

  Examples:

  - When Spencer stood near a magnetron, a vacuum tube that generates microwaves to boost the sensitivity of radar, he noted an odd sensation; the chocolate bar in his pocket had melted, and a bag of popcorn popped. A year later he had patented the technology for a microwave oven (e.g., Leslie, 2012);

  - George de Mestral was out walking his dog when he noted the prickly seeds from shrubs that got caught in the fabric of his clothes, which led him to wonder why which they stick, and after investigation to go on to invent Velcro (e.g., Pease et al., 2013)

  Neither reportedly set out to solve the problems; they made astute observations which when combined with their own knowledge led to surprise outcomes.

- Type B. *From Problem I to a Solution for Problem II*

In this variation, an individual is looking for a solution to a problem, but instead finds a solution to another problem. This is the interpretation of Solly and the literary scholars of the 19th century (and it was interpretation that was first quoted in the Oxford English Dictionary in 1913) and continues to be perhaps the most popular interpretation today.

Examples:

○ Fleming was growing Staphylococcus bacteria in a petri dish when it became contaminated with a spore of Penicilliusm fungus. His deep understanding of bacteria (his sagacity) led him to observe how the mold in his petri dish killed the surrounding bacteria, and thus led to one of the most important advancements in health in the early 20th century (e.g., Roberts, 1989);

○ Art Fry was trying to develop a superglue when he accidentally devised a very weak glue that enabled two pieces of paper to be pried apart which led to development of Post-it Notes (e.g., Pease et al., 2013).

In both these cases, the researchers were working diligently on a particular problem when an observation led them in a different direction, resulting in a novel solution to a problem that they had not initially intended to solve.

• Type C. *Unexpected Solutions*

An individual is looking for a solution to a particular problem, but the solution does not come from expected sources. The solution discovered by accident is found in an unusual or surprising way that could not have been predicted at the outset. This has also been called pseudo-serendipity (Roberts, 1989).

Example:

○ Goodyear was seeking a solution to the problem of rubber. In winter it hardened, while in summer it melted. As the story goes, he accidentally dropped rubber on a stove and observed on cooling that it turned into a charred leather-like substance with an elastic rim. From this unexpected event, he invented vulcanized rubber that is still in use today (e.g., Halacy, 1967).

Serendipity Types A, B, and C share common features as illustrated in Figure 1.1. In their examination of serendipity, de Figueiredo and Campos (2001) provide a parsimonious mathematical notation to describe each. The types are typically distinguished by whether there was intent to solve a problem or find a solution to a new or existing problem (Napier and Vuong, 2013; Foster and Ford, 2003; Cunha et al, 2014; De Rond, 2014). All types emerge out of a context, which may be any work or pleasure environment, with variable starting points, and all get to a solution; if this were the only ingredients, then we would be dealing with ordinary problem-solving. What distinguishes these types from ordinary problem solving are the two key points in the process:

- the startling, anomalous observation(s); that leads to

- an unexpected, unpredictable outcome.

These elements, thus, become the defining characteristics that separate the ordinary from the serendipitous.

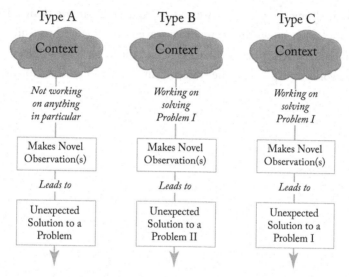

Figure 1.1: Three ways serendipity happens.

1.4   WHAT DO WE MEAN BY SERENDIPITY IN DIGITAL INFORMATION ENVIRONMENTS?

A digital information environment can be any piece of digital technology that enables a "sense of place" and enables user interaction with information objects (McCay-Peet, Toms, and Kelloway, 2014). This may be any software application, from desktop to the Web. How does this environment differ from those in which we typically discuss serendipity? Most examples from science and engineering described earlier deal with human interactions with *physical* objects that have visually revealing characteristics, e.g., mold, burrs, floppy ears, burning rubber. When the anomalous or unexpected observation occurs in a two-dimensional digital space such as a computer, tablet or phone display, those anomalous and unexpected cues emanate from a combination of text, icons, images and sounds that make up an information object, and thus must be cognitively interpreted. There are (at present) no tangible tactile elements in a digital environment. In this volume, it is this digital environment in which we explore serendipity.

1.5   REST OF THE BOOK

In the remainder of the volume we consider the motivation for researching serendipity, and the value and implications for doing so. In Chapter 2, we examine why it is pertinent and timely to study serendipity. In Chapter 3, we deconstruct the concept of serendipity, and consider its use and interpretation, e.g., as an event, a behavior, a process, an outcome. In Chapter 4, we consider how to facilitate it in digital environments, answering the question can we design for serendipity. In Chapters 5 and 6, we look at how various methods have been deployed to study it and how it has been or could be assessed when it has occurred. We end the book with a reflection of the research to date and a framework for explaining the concept, thus providing a basis for future research.

CHAPTER 2

What Drives Serendipity Research?

Reasons for examining the phenomenon of serendipity have evolved and grown over the past 25 years. Rapid technological change has provided both impetus and inspiration for serendipity research that examines how people adopt, adapt to, use, and, in turn, influence digital environments and how to design them to better support serendipity in the context of learning, everyday life, business, scholarship, law, and leisure, to name a few. The purpose of this chapter is to gather the main drivers of serendipity research, which point to responses to the proverbial "so what?" question.

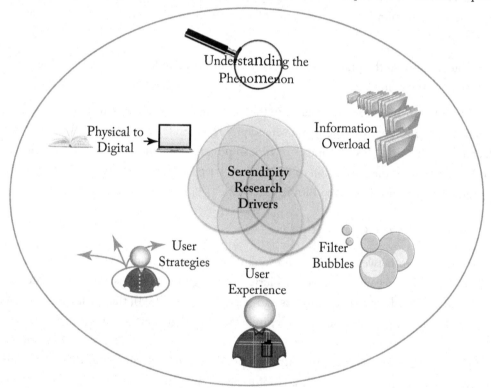

Figure 2.1: Six main drivers of serendipity research relating to digital information environments.

We identified six main, overlapping drivers of serendipity research relating to digital information environments (Figure 2.1).

- **Physical vs. digital:** Compare serendipity-related benefits of digital and physical interactions or mimic characteristics of physical environments to support serendipity in digital environments.

- **Information overload:** Develop digital environments that enable users to encounter triggers of serendipitous experiences in the face of information overload.

- **Filter bubbles:** Burst "filter bubbles" through novel approaches to support serendipity.

- **User experience:** Understand and foster the positive experiences associated with serendipity to benefit individuals, groups, networks, and society.

- **User strategies:** Identify how users may increase opportunities for serendipity through their information behavior or frame of mind in their interactions with digital environments.

- **Understanding the phenomenon:** Gain a theoretical understanding of the phenomenon of serendipity.

Although not always explicitly stated in the research, these six drivers are tied to even broader incentives: the implications of support for serendipity reverberate politically, socially, economically, and technologically through serendipity's relationship to, for example, learning, community building, and innovation. In the conclusion of this chapter we both summarize the research drivers and suggest others to which it has yet to turn its attention.

2.1   PHYSICAL VS. DIGITAL

While the separation between "offline" and "online" or "virtual world" and "real world" networks and communities has become increasingly blurred, and arguments against the very existence of a division were proposed more than 10 years ago (e.g., Wellman, 2004), the qualities of interaction among people, information, and objects differ in physical vs. digital environments. The *serendipitous sociocognitive microenvironment* (Merton and Barber, 2004) needs, at the very least, some massaging when considering the relatively recent shift from physical to digital. Since the 1990s, research has examined how interactions with people and information differ in physical vs. digital environments and whether the positive, serendipitous aspects of physical environment may be mimicked or augmented through our interactions with digital environments.

Discussion relating to the shift from physical to digital and its implications on serendipity and how digital can either replace or enhance our physical interactions is evident, for example, in relation to the shift from physical to digital photography, in approaches to humanities research, and the development of collaborative work environments. Research has sought to find ways in which digital photographs may be remembered and shared as easily, or perhaps more so, than their physical counterparts (Frohlich, Wall, and Kiddle, 2013; Nunes, Greenberg, and Neustaedter, 2009). Findings relating to serendipity in the humanities suggest unease over the shift from physical to digital source materials, although Verhoeven and de Costa (2014) note that this may dissipate with time through new methodological approaches and technological changes. Currently, however, among historians, research suggests that while more and more artifacts and manuscripts are becoming digitally accessible, there is apprehension that the shift from physical books to eBooks may reduce opportunity for serendipity rather than support it (Quan-Haase and Martin, 2012; Martin and Quan-Haase, 2013, 2016). In serendipity research relating to work or enterprise, the emphasis is often on co-workers' information-rich interactions with each other and how the phenomenon may be facilitated by enabling informal online communication (e.g., Guy et al., 2015; Whittaker, Frohlich, and Daly-Jones, 1994). We focus in the remainder of this section on the work or enterprise area of research where the motivation for serendipity research has a distinctly physical vs. digital perspective: Computer-Supported Cooperative Work (CSCW).

Early CSCW research (e.g., Whittaker, Frohlich, and Daly-Jones, 1994) was motivated by findings indicating that physical proximity has a significant influence on opportunistic collaboration among researchers (Kraut, Egido, and Galegher, 1988). Researchers at Hewlett Packard, for example, examined how informal communication, including communication prompted by "chance encounters," could in some way be replicated online to support geographically distributed groups (Whittaker, Frohlich, and Daly-Jones, 1994). Jeffrey (2000) examined whether chance encounters occur in a "networked, virtual world with three-dimensional avatar representation" (p. 331) and found that chance encounters known to occur in physical environments can be reproduced in virtual environments. CSCW continues to examine how to support serendipity through, for example, updates on fellow employees' social media activity (Guy et al., 2015) and the implications of serendipitous experiences in work environments such as enhanced communication and productivity (Brown et al., 2014).

While researchers and developers are forging ahead with the development of approaches to increase the potential for serendipity in digital information environments, there is a recognition that technological support for serendipity is not quite "there yet," as evidenced from moves by technologically sophisticated companies such as Yahoo!, Google, and IBM to encourage face-to-face interactions among its employees (e.g., Lindsay, 2014; Silverman, 2013; Wolsen, 2013). Yahoo! made news in 2013 when CEO Marissa Mayer barred employees from working from home, a move widely held to be associated with the desire to increase productivity as well as the belief that serendipity, a driver of innovation, was more likely to occur through diverse, face-to-face interactions with colleagues than at one's home office or through online communication (Wolsen, 2013). Because face-to-face interactions were credited with innovations at the search engine giant Google, including Gmail and Street View, the company designed its headquarters to ensure its employees could, according to a Google spokesperson, "collaborate and bump into each other" (Silverman, 2013, n.p.). Similarly, IBM's Accelerated Discovery Lab, with its open space and dynamic concept, was designed to ensure "cross-pollination" among colleagues from different disciplines and teams and visitors to the lab would have opportunities to interact with each other and big data. Laura Haas, the lab's director of technology and operations, noted

> *We call it cultivating "strategic serendipity." It's those "A-ha!" moments you have in the shower or often around the water cooler. We want to bring people together in a rich enough environment they want to play in it, and then create serendipity by leveraging the connections in the room, the connections in the data, and our ability to see what users are doing* (Lindsay, 2014, n.p.).

Currently, without a better alternative, high-tech companies continue to recognize the need for face-to-face interactions to facilitate serendipity. Regardless, however, of the push to get colleagues in the same room together through company policies and architectural design, a significant amount of worker interactions with data, information, and knowledge now take place online, through email, social media, search engines, databases, and other digital information resources and sources. Therefore, the need to get serendipity "right" in digital information environments is critical and continues to be a prime motivation for serendipity research.

2.2   INFORMATION OVERLOAD

One of the main benefits of digital information environments is the plethora of dynamic, diverse, and hyperlinked information that those environments contain, with the potential to trigger serendipitous experiences. At the same time, some argue that this type of information-rich environment is just as likely to spur information overload as it is to trigger serendipity—arguably more so. This tension between the need to manage both the quantity and quality of information has been a key driver of serendipity research. How can digital environments provide a balance between manageable information exposure and drawing attention to information that may be considered unexpected but useful (i.e., serendipitous)? Relative to the information overload phenomenon, associated with enterprise time and money (Barta, 2014; International Data Corporation, 2001) as well as anxiety and stress (Erdelez, 1996; Yadamsuren and Heinström, 2011), a serendipitous digital environment must meet the demands of user experience like any other digital environment otherwise people will not stay or return (Åman et al., 2014).

Information overload is a term "often used to convey the simple notion of *receiving too much information*" (Eppler and Mengis, 2004, p. 326). Research across a variety of disciplines indicates that the quality of individuals' decisions correlates with the amount of information received, but only up to a point. Once that threshold is reached, information overload ensues as information can no longer be integrated into decision-making (Eppler and Mengis, 2004). Eppler and Mengis describe the inverted U-curve associated with this relationship between decision-making and information load, first articulated by Schroder, Driver, and Streufert (1967). In serendipity research, information overload is often referred to in related terms; a similar U-curve schematic can be imagined in which "decision-making" is replaced by "serendipity." The more information provided in a digital information environment, the more opportunity for serendipity—but still, *up to a point*. Figure 2.2 illustrates the relationship between serendipity and information load that is often articulated in serendipity research as a phenomenon to be wary of and to limit by design (e.g., Bellotti et al., 2008; Cleverley and Burnett, 2015a; Guy et al., 2015; Rädle et al., 2012).

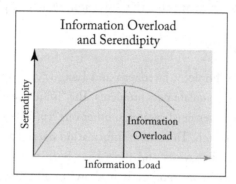

Figure 2.2: Serendipity relative to information load; "decision making" replaced by "serendipity" (adapted from Eppler and Mengis, 2004).

Serendipity research often seeks to address information overload by exploring how information presented to users may be a combination of both serendipity as well as accuracy, often operationalized as unexpected *and* interesting or relevant information. For example, to prevent information overload without too narrowly defining the scope of what to present to users, Ruxanda, Nanopoulos, and Jensen (2010) balanced the criteria used to rank music retrieval results, which included serendipity, authority, importance, and relevance, rather than simply audio similarity. Syndicating enterprise social media streams has also been proposed to both reduce information overload among enterprise employees while also ensuring that employees are more apt to both view relevant content and have their content viewed by interested people (Guy et al., 2015).

Providing options to users has also been proposed to give people some agency over how they would like to deal with the problem of information overload and, ultimately, to explicitly indicate their openness to serendipity at any given moment. For example, users may choose "serendipitous" over "known-item" search (Pittarello, 2004), indicate desired level of surprise in recommendations (Guy et al., 2015), control the level of diversity of suggestions (Benjamin, et al. 2014), change search parameters to shuffle and dynamically reorder event results (Nielsen et al., 2015), or have the power to turn context filtering for recommendations on or off (Bellotti et al., 2008). Similarly, transparency, indicating to users why, for example, a song has been recommended is also important when presenting less obvious, potentially more serendipitous, recommendations (Hornung et al., 2013).

While information overload is a common motivation for serendipity research, not all agree that information overload is a problem. De Bruijn and Spence (2008), for example, argue that, given the human capacity to rapidly process information (and forget it), rather than trying to avoid information overload, people need to be exposed to a large amount of information. This exposure is necessary if the goal is to increase opportunities for serendipitous access to information, balancing the need for personalization with the need to enable serendipitous interaction (Fan et al., 2012). Concern that people may be missing out on serendipitous opportunities because of filtering technology is precisely what led to another primary motivation for serendipity research: filter bubbles.

2.3   FILTER BUBBLES

In their research on mobile technology, Jarvenpaa and Lang (2005) found that while technology provides solutions, it also tends to create new problems. The "fulfills needs/creates needs" paradox—"the same feature that fulfills a user need creates another one" (p. 13)—is evident in relation to the drive to support information search. To combat information overload, approaches to filtering and personalization and push-back behaviors and tools have been proposed (Morrison and Gomez, 2014). But with advancements in technology that allow for filtering and personalization, come concern for the "filter bubbles" they may create (Pariser, 2011). Indeed, while filtering and personalization may help alleviate the problem of information overload, they are creating the potential for another problem: exposure to a narrow selection of information and ideas with which the user likely agrees or is already aware (Pariser, 2011). What are people missing out on when their searches are filtered and they are only exposed to the information, news, ideas, and products that conform to their location and click and search history (i.e., interests and beliefs)? Serendipity research is motivated not only to address the filter bubble problem (e.g., Benjamin et al., 2014; Kirman, Linehan, and Lawson, 2012) but also to investigate whether this concern is well-founded (e.g., André, Teevan, and Dumais, 2009b). The latter, however, is often assumed, which makes it difficult to know the extent of the filter bubble problem.

The debate around filter bubbles, however, is not only an academic one. Filter bubbles (Pariser, 2011) have been cited by the media in the aftermath of major political events such as the 2016 referendum in the United Kingdom (Bell, 2016) and the 2016 American presidential election (Rose-Stockwell, 2016) as the reason why so many were surprised with the outcomes. Those who felt the vote would be "no" to the U.K.'s withdrawal from the European Union (Brexit) and that Hillary Clinton rather than Donald Trump would win the presidential election in the US in 2016 were at least partially getting this impression through the echo chambers they were inhabiting through their social media platforms. They were only hearing from people who shared their opinions and were exposed to the same news and information. Filter bubbles, it was proposed, may ultimately curtail exposure to diverse, novel information and ideas, and impact the potential for serendipity with political ramifications.

Filtering has been used for some time as a method of coping with information overload, focusing on specific, important information and the avoidance of unimportant information (Savolainen, 2007). In the context of search engines, "important information" is essentially precise or accurate search results. Research (e.g., André et al., 2009b; Forsblom et al., 2012; Huldtgren et al., 2014; Kirman et al., 2012; Maksai et al., 2015; Matt et al., 2014; Taramigkou et al., 2013; Zhang et al., 2012) has noted that improving the accuracy of search results and recommendations through filtering does not necessarily lead to better search experiences and these "improvements" have broad social and political implications (Pariser, 2011; Zuckerman, 2011). Forsblum et al. (2012) argue, for example, that people tend to be fed content that is similar to the content they are usually exposed to or content that is popular rather than novel or potentially serendipitous. André et al. (2009b) similarly indicate that personalization "may reduce opportunities for serendipity on the Web" (p. 2033), though ultimately argue that personalization may also be used to support serendipity. Huldtgren et al. (2014) suggests there has been a decline in serendipitous experiences that have the potential to broaden people's perspectives not only due to filtering but also "an acceleration of everyday life through technology" (n.p.). Also concerning, Guy et al. (2015) found that while their personalization method for item recommendation within an enterprise social stream did not intend for personalized items to be predominantly authored by employees of the same country as their readers, they nonetheless found this algorithmic bias. All of these examples suggest the need to carefully examine how changes to digital environments interact with other factors and impact users.

The FOMO (fear-of-missing-out) phenomenon has been channeled by serendipity researchers who are eager to ensure that while information overload is stemmed, it is not at the expense of serendipity. Evidence of FOMO was found in a serendipity-related study (Nielsen et al., 2015) in which participants wrongly assumed that sliders that allowed users to control the parameters of urban events were acting as filters, preventing them from seeing all possible events. Users need to know that the system is showing them *all* relevant events. Stemming FOMO is evident in Benjamin et al.'s (2014) motivation behind the development of Juxtapose, described as a "clipart composition workflow" (p. 342). Juxtapose was designed to both help users navigate the deluge of images available online and to ensure that the image retrieval algorithms, which have become very accurate in recent years, do not eliminate serendipity from the image search process. While algorithms are getting increasingly better at accuracy, pulling information that has the potential to spark serendipity may be a far greater challenge than selecting accurate information because the approach risks annoying users if the results are consistently neither accurate nor serendipitous (André et al., 2009a).

Matt et al. (2014), however, recognizing the trade-off between providing recommendations that are relevant and perhaps even known to users and recommendations that do not fit their previously noted preferences, tested the notion that people would want to break out of their filter bubbles. In their study on recommender systems in which 130 university students participated in a web-based field experiment, Matt et al. found that simply providing novel recommendations was not enough because of the cost novelty had to the perception of "preference fit"; rather, users were open to serendipitous recommendations, those that were both valuable *and* surprising, ultimately aligning with their interests and providing enjoyment. Regardless, filter bubbles continue to be a topic of discussion in the popular press and a driver of serendipity research.

2.4   USER EXPERIENCE

While serendipity is generally associated with positive experiences, serendipity involves work to reach some of the possible valuable outcomes of the experience (McCay-Peet and Toms, 2015) and thus serendipity is not always welcome. People may want to avoid serendipitous experiences due to time constraints (Makri et al., 2014; McBirnie, 2008; Sun et al., 2011) or stress and anxiety (Heinström, 2006; Yadamsuren and Heinström, 2011). Moreover, interest and relevance are dynamic rather than static, changing over time and through context (André et al., 2009b); stumbling upon a useful, unexpected search result may be considered serendipitous one day but not if it was found the very next day when the need has passed. Recognizing its time- and context-sensitive elements, some systems designed to support serendipity have been developed to allow for tasks to be deferred (Ahn and Pierce, 2005) to help improve user experience. With all its potential to drive some people away, serendipity is generally considered a positive experience and, by extension, a positive user experience.

All three of the preceding drivers of serendipity research in digital environments (physical to digital; information overload; filter bubbles) are tied to user experience; they all underscore a determination to improve "a person's perceptions and responses resulting from the use and/or anticipated use of a product, system or service" (International Organization for Standardization [ISO], 2010, p. 3). The first driver outlined in this chapter (Section 2.1) focuses on the ongoing transition from physical to digital and the latter two (Sections 2.2 and 2.3) have been largely tied to pervasive problems relating to technological developments that have the potential to negatively impact user experience: information overload and filter bubbles. However, the ISO (2010) provides three notes on its definition of user experience that point to a myriad of factors that influence user experience including users' goals, attitudes, prior states, and system functionality and usability. In this section, we highlight the aspect of user experience that "includes all the users' emotions, beliefs, preferences, perceptions, physical and psychological responses, behaviors and accomplishments that occur before, during and after use" (p. 3). Serendipity research has framed the valuable outcomes of a serendipitous experience as personal, organizational or community, or global (McCay-Peet and

Toms, 2015). Serendipity research relating to digital environments tends to focus on the first two, which are explored below.

Personal outcomes. On the level of personal outcomes or impact of support for serendipity, research examining how to improve user experience varies considerably. For example, serendipity research has explored how to enhance user experience relating to search (e.g., Bordino et al., 2014), sightseeing (Bellotti et al., 2008), and music selection and listening (e.g., Liikkanen and Åman, 2016; Leong, Vetere, and Howard, 2005; Leong et al., 2010). Bordino et al. (2014) argue the objective of modern search engines has evolved and is not only to deliver a set of documents but also an *engaging* experience that can stimulate creative thinking; serendipity is one way to keep users "interacting with the system even without a predefined purpose" (p. 2). Leong et al. (2010) found through their research on serendipity, digital music, and user experience "that at the heart of the experience of serendipity was the emergence of powerful personal meanings out of seemingly random coincidence of events" (p. 263). Zhang et al. (2012) found that by ensuring their music recommender system, Auralist, supported serendipity, they were able to improve user satisfaction, an important aspect of user experience.

Organizational or community outcomes. Advancements in technology that support serendipity have also been motivated by the desire to improve strength of family bonds (e.g., Bentley et al., 2011) or to understand the "serendipity of place" (Hristova et al., 2016). Bentley et al.'s (2011) *Serendipitous Family Stories System* was designed to encourage "communication across generations and enhance[e] users' relationships with everyday places in their lives" (p. 31). A sense of community in geographically distributed workforces is partially dependent on opportunities for both casual and chance encounters among members (Renduchintala, 2006). Hristova et al. (2016) note that due to the ever-increasing number of people living in urban areas, urban planners as well as systems designers need to understand the affect that human mobility has on urban diversity; just how serendipitous a place is, "the extent to which it can induce chance encounters between its visitors" (p. 23) is an important aspect of social diversity.

2.5   USER STRATEGIES

While much of the research on serendipity in digital environments focuses on how user interfaces, mobile applications, and search and recommender system algorithms can facilitate serendipity (e.g., Taramigkou et al., 2017), there is a small body of research that examines the user side of this equation. While technology can be designed to provide opportunities for serendipity, namely, digital environments conducive to serendipitous experiences, the user also has a role to play; the user can adopt strategies, approaches, behaviors, or frames of mind when interacting with digital environments to increase the chances of experiencing serendipity. Stewart and Basic (2014) found that undergraduate students were failing to take advantage of their information encounters—they were not following up to ensure the valuable outcomes associated with serendipity despite the existence of built-in web tools to help them capture the information for later use. They concluded that undergraduate students needed information literacy training to understand how to "manage and retrieve unexpected information while using the internet" (p. 74). The process of a serendipitous experience is influenced by both environmental and human factors (e.g., Erdelez, 1996; Merton and Barber, 2004) and both must be taken into consideration in the development of serendipitous digital environments. To this end, another driver of serendipity research in the context of digital information environments relates to the development of strategies to enable users to increase the likelihood of serendipity.

While there is some evidence of a link between the personality trait of extraversion and serendipity (McCay-Peet, Toms, and Kelloway, 2015) and incidental information acquisition (IIA) (Heinström, 2006), the approaches and strategies users take or apply to their interactions with information in digital environments appear to hold the most promise in complementing the development of serendipitous digital information environments. Heinström (2006), for example, found that intrinsic motivation and engagement had a positive relationship to IIA—students in three separate studies who employed a "deep approach" to studying in which they built on their comprehension with each new piece of information were more likely to experience IIA. Search style, something that can be taught, is also associated with serendipity. Heinström (2006) found that broad scanning, "a search style where a topic is spontaneously explored through a wide use of sources" (p. 587) was positively associated with IIA, unlike deep diving, which requires a high level of focus, and fast surfing, in which little effort is exerted in the information seeking process. Erdelez (1996) points out the potential for "non-encounters," those who do not currently experience the positive implications of information encountering, to model the behavior or approaches of "super-encounters" who are sensitive to information in their environment while avoiding the pitfalls of information overload.

Taking a different tack, Makri et al. (2014) explored how strategies may inform the design of serendipity digital environments. Through interviews with 14 creative professionals, they explored the strategies that professionals reported they used to increase their likelihood of serendipity. Makri et al. (2014) noted several strategies through which they identified how current digital environments support serendipity and how the creative professionals' strategies may in turn inform the development of environments that support serendipity. It seems investigating user strategies that increase opportunity for serendipity may not only inform information literacy training but also help improve digital information environments, enhancing their ability to support serendipity. Rahman and Wilson (2015) note, for example, the possibility of supporting two types of search behavior—"casual searching" and "focused work tasks" through the design of serendipitous user interfaces.

2.6   UNDERSTANDING THE PHENOMENON

Finally, understanding the phenomenon—investigating the theoretical underpinnings of serendipity—is a key motivation for serendipity research. This line of inquiry, which seeks to understand how serendipity unfolds, what influences it, and its implications through the development of models and frameworks, provides the ground work for research on serendipity to develop. Models and frameworks in the area of information needs, behavior, and use as well as the computational context have been developed to explain serendipity, propose recommendations and heuristics to practitioners, and help point to gaps in the literature.

The phenomenon of serendipity, despite its information-rich nature, has been largely absent from *general* information models and frameworks relating to information needs, seeking, and use. While parts of the experience of serendipity are captured in information models such as Ellis' (2005) information seeking behavior, and Dervin's (Dervin and Foreman-Wernet, 2003) sense making models, "no single general model of information explains serendipity" (McCay-Peet and Toms, 2015, p. 1464). Models and frameworks have sought to put the spotlight on the phenomenon or aspects of the phenomenon to help explain, for example, information encountering (Erdelez, 1997; 2005), incidental information acquisition in everyday life (Williamson, 1998), everyday chance encounters (Rubin, Burkell, and Quan-Haase, 2011), the nature of serendipity in information research (Sun et al., 2011), the process of serendipity (Makri and Blandford, 2012; McCay-Peet and Toms, 2015), and micro-serendipity (Boger and Björneborn, 2013).

Several models of the process or experience of serendipity have been developed and are discussed in Chapter 3 (also see Table 3.1); there are more similarities than differences among them. While different models and frameworks place different emphasis on the various elements of the phenomenon due to context (e.g., recommender systems, search, social media, everyday life), they all help to build consensus on the main elements of the phenomenon which is useful not only to future research but to practitioners trying to find ways to support serendipity. Serendipity research, however, is still in its infancy, and understanding the phenomenon will continue to be a primary research driver.

2.7   SUMMARY

The treatment of technology and its relationship with serendipity has changed in the past 25 years, moving from a broad conceptualization of opportunities for serendipity in physical versus digital information environments to a more nuanced approach that reflects the increasing complexity of technology and our interactions with and perceptions of it. This chapter discussed six overlapping drivers of serendipity research as they have been articulated to date: (1) map physical to digital; (2) reduce information overload; (3) burst filter bubbles; (4) improve user experience; (5) identify user strategies to facilitate serendipitous experiences; and (6) understand the phenomenon in order to build theory, provide recommendations to practitioners, and identify gaps in the research. There will likely be more motivations for serendipity research on the horizon as digital information environments and the nature and degree of their use continue to evolve.

It is important to note that underlying the six drivers in relation to the research on serendipity in digital environments is the notion that digital environments have the potential to facilitate serendipity and some may do it better than others (e.g., Cleverley and Burnett, 2015a; McCay-Peet, Toms, and Kelloway, 2015). However, owing to the complexity of context, serendipity in digital environments may be viewed by users as either good or bad so extra care must be taken for its support. Moreover, while tools may be designed to support serendipity, they are doing so because it is believed that support for serendipity is a means to an end—a way to ensure, for example, good user experience, the bursting of filter bubbles, and the identification of positive user strategies. One of the lessons of serendipity research is that trying to solve a problem may create new ones, therefore, research must be conscious of the impact "improvements" are having. For example, what are the ethical implications of facilitating serendipity? We know algorithms are not neutral; what ethical issues do systems that purport to facilitate serendipity raise? The ethics of support for serendipity has yet to be fully explored. What forms of algorithmic bias should we be aware of in relation to support for serendipity? Are systems designed to support serendipity (e.g., by presenting diverse recommendations) more ethical than those that narrowly define interests (see, for example, Jones, 2015)? What are the privacy implications of personalization designed to support serendipity; is the tradeoff worth it? Research on serendipity rarely addresses these broader ethical issues (exceptions include, for example, Hangal, Nagpal, and Lam, 2012).

CHAPTER 3

Approaches to Serendipity

While dichotomized as either a personal aptitude or a phenomenon or event (Merton and Barber, 2004), a review of the serendipity research relating to digital environments reveals that serendipity is primarily approached as either a

1. *quality* of an event, something, or someone; or a

2. *process or experience*, which has one or more serendipitous qualities.

Serendipity as a process or experience is the most holistic approach to serendipity, capturing not only the moment of discovery or realization but what triggered the experience and followed, all centered around the person who experienced it. On the other hand, approached as a quality, four main types are discernable, including the qualities of

- *an event* (e.g., the act of stumbling upon a useful link);

- *something* (e.g., a useful and unexpected search result or recommendation); or

- *someone* (e.g., the openness of an individual to an unexpected experience or event; a fruitful search tactic that prompts serendipity)

What is most apparent in a review of the prior research on serendipity in the context of digital environments is that serendipity is often approached as a process or experience in information science and human-computer interaction research (Makri and Blandford, 2012; McCay-Peet and Toms, 2015; Rubin, Burkell, and Quan-Haase, 2011; Sun et al., 2011) or a quality of someone in information behavior research (e.g., Yadamsuren and Erdelez, 2010, 2016). However, in research relating to recommender systems and search engines, serendipity is most often approached as a quality of an event or something, with research effectively carving off a specific aspect of the process or experience to take a closer look and solve a specific problem (exceptions include Corneli, et al., 2016; Taramigkou, Apostolou, and Mentzas, 2017).

The distinctions among the various approaches are important; namely, they reveal what underlying factors are hypothesized to contribute to serendipity or, at the very least, the primary focus of the research at hand. Each of the various ways in which serendipity has been interpreted in research adds to an understanding of the phenomenon, draws attention to one or more of its facets, and helps explain how it may be facilitated. The following sections explore serendipity first as a process or experience and then as a quality in its four main forms.

3.1   SERENDIPITY AS A PROCESS OR EXPERIENCE

Serendipity is sometimes characterized holistically as an *experience*, "the process of doing and seeing things and of having things happen to you" (Experience, n.d.). Several models of the process or experience of serendipity have emerged in recent years, driven primarily by the motivation to understand serendipity and what might facilitate it relating to its various elements or stages. From research focusing on serendipity in both digital and non-digital information environments, the phenomenon is generally approached as a process or experience to understand serendipity from the user's perspective rather than a strictly systems approach (e.g., Corneli, et al., 2016; Makri and Blandford, 2012; McCay-Peet and Toms, 2015; Rubin et al., 2011; Sun et al., 2011). Table 3.1 outlines the main elements of serendipity models.

What is evident from an analysis of the elements of various serendipity models (Table 3.1) is that there is a great deal of agreement among the models of what constitutes serendipity. Three main stages are evident in most of the models: (1) trigger/connection; (2) follow-up; and (3) valuable outcome/reflection. The trigger/connection and valuable outcome elements are present in all five models in one form or another. Something or someone must be the catalyst for the experience (i.e., *trigger*), the user must make a *connection* between the trigger and their knowledge or experience (i.e., prepared mind), and it must have a *valuable outcome* because, after all, serendipity is by nature a positive experience. While framed in different ways, the chance or unexpectedness of the experience, critical to the definition of serendipity, is also noted in each model. Three of the five models include perception or consideration of serendipity or reflection on the experience or reframing of events (Makri and Blandford, 2012; McCay-Peet and Toms, 2015; Rubin et al., 2011). Perception or reflection is important in the context of support for digital environments; applications, websites, recommender systems, etc. may be designed to facilitate serendipity, but do they succeed from a user perspective? Three of the five models also include some sort of follow-up or bridge to the valuable outcome (Corneli, et al., 2016; Makri and Blandford, 2012; McCay-Peet and Toms, 2015), underlining the importance of work to reach a valuable outcome as well as the need to provide features in digital environments to support follow-up, for example sharing features first noted almost two decades ago by Erdelez and Rioux (2000a, 2000b) relative to information encountering.

What needs to be augmented in models and frameworks of serendipity are the factors that influence the process or experience. Qualities and characteristics relating to each of the main elements all hold the key to filling out and ultimately helping to combine models of serendipity from various fields of research. The following section outlines the three main qualities identified in the research—serendipity as a quality of an event, something, or someone. The serendipitous qualities of something (e.g., recommendations, search results) and event, for example, help explain the trigger and connections elements of the process, while serendipitous qualities of someone may help

Table 3.1: Main elements in selected serendipity models and frameworks

Serendipity Models	Linear or quasi-linear elements of the process*						Nonlinear elements*
Corneli et al. (2016)	Prepared mind	Trigger	Focus shift	Bridge	Result		Dimensions: chance, curiosity, sagacity, value
Makri and Blandford (2012)	Make new connection (involving unexpected circumstances and insight)			Project potential value; Exploit connection	Valuable, unanticipated outcome	Reflect on value of outcome / unexpectedness of circumstance; Consider as serendipity	
McCay-Peet et al. (2015)	Trigger	Connection (possibly delayed)	Follow-up		Valuable outcome	Perception of serendipity	Unexpected thread; internal and external factors
Rubin et al. (2011)	Facets A, B, C related to the Find — Facet A: Prepared mind	Facet B: Act of noticing	Facet C: Chance		Facet D: Fortuitous outcome (perceived gain/happy ending)	Re-framing events, story retold	
Sun et al., (2011)	Noticing; Examining; Unexpected finding of information	Making connections			Value of serendipity		Context (social, physical, time, user)

*Note. Linear elements progress from element to element, though this progression is often linear in nature. Nonlinear elements refer to factors that may affect or relate to multiple main elements or indicate that different parts of the process or experience of serendipity are iterative.

explain different part of the process, for example, how the trigger is encountered (e.g., search style), prepared mind, and whether the experience is perceived serendipitous.

3.2   SERENDIPITY AS A QUALITY

Serendipity is most often treated in the research as "a characteristic or feature that someone or something has: something that can be noticed as a part of a person or a thing" (Quality, n.d.); more specifically, as a quality of an event, something, or someone. By far, however, more research has examined serendipity as a quality of an *event* or *something* due to the proliferation of literature relating to search engines and recommender systems in which serendipitous is used to describe initial "events" that take place within the process of serendipity (e.g., information encounters) or "things" such as search results and recommendations. Less common is serendipity approached in research relating to digital environments as a quality of *someone*; the focus of serendipity research tends to be more systems than user-centric in the sense that much of the research is about how serendipity may be supported by creating, for example, search user interfaces, *for* users rather than understanding qualities of the users themselves (e.g., personality, whether they are prone to serendipity) or what the user may bring to the table (e.g., their strategies for experiencing serendipity; search behaviors). The sections to follow describe the treatment of serendipity as an event, something, or someone throughout the literature of serendipity in digital environments.

Quality of an event. Most formal definitions of serendipity describe serendipity as an occurrence, an event, "something, (especially something important or notable) that happens" (Event, n.d.). Serendipity, in this vein, is often a quality of an encounter (e.g., Åman et al., 2014), an interaction (Jeffrey, 2000), a discovery (e.g., Bordino et al., 2014), or a specific type of event or interaction—a conversation (e.g., Inkpen et al., 2008). Words like event, accident, interaction, exposure, acquisition, and discovery are often used interchangeably with the same research papers to describe serendipity. Åman et al. (2014) define serendipity in the context of their research on music recommendations as "random *encounters* of good or useful content unexpectedly" (p. 62, emphasis added) and also describe as "serendipitous music discoveries" (p. 69). Some research focuses on the information behavior that underlines these events rather than the event itself (e.g., Erdelez's [2004] information encountering); this research is discussed in a forthcoming section on serendipity as a quality of someone.

Defining serendipity as an event is most evident in research in the computer sciences where operationalizing an aspect of the experience of serendipity is necessary to solve a specific problem, such how to trigger serendipity (e.g., André et al., 2009b). Another pattern that became apparent was that when serendipity was defined as an event, it would often be subsequently treated as a quality of something (e.g., Liikkanen and Åman, 2016). Table 3.2 includes a selection of ways in which serendipity has been approached as an event in the research.

Table 3.2: Examples of research in which serendipity is approached as a quality of an event

Quality of an Event	
Event or accident	
"**events** with fortuitous outcomes arising from chance or accidents"	Leong et al. (2010)
"the **accident** of finding something good or useful without looking for it"	Said et al. (2012)
Encounter, interaction, exposure, or acquisition	
"random **encounters** of good or useful content unexpectedly, i.e., serendipity"	Åman et al. (2014)
"serendipitous **encounters**"	Rahman and Wilson (2015)
"unexpected but welcome **encounter**"	Liikkanen and Åman (2016)
"unplanned **interaction**"; "chance **encounters**";	Jeffrey (2000)
"positively surprising observations of things we were not looking for, i.e. serendipitous **encounters**"	Huldtgren et al. (2014)
"Online information **encountering**"	Jiang, Lui, and Chi (2015)
"Serendipity, or the act of unexpectedly **encountering** something fortunate	André et al. (2009b)
"*serendipitous* **acquisition** [...] occurs when a user's gaze happens to fall on a representation [...] of some information of interest"	De Bruijn and Spence (2008)
Discovery	
"serendipitous music **discoveries**"	Åman et al. (2014)
"'shape serendipity' is the chance **discovery** of shapes"	Benjamin et al. (2014)
"a **discovery** of something new and interesting"	Bordino et al. (2014)
"fortuitous unexpected information **discovery**"	Cleverley and Burnett (2015a)
"serendipitous **discovery** of photos"	Frohlich, Wall, and Kiddle (2013)
"Serendipitous conversation and photo **discovery**"	Nunes, Greenberg, Neustaedter (2009)
"serendipitous **discoveries**"	Rädle et al. (2012); Rahman and Wilson (2015)
Conversation	
"serendipitous group **conversations**"	Inkpen et al. (2008)
"Serendipitous **conversation** and photo discovery"	Nunes, Greenberg, Neustaedter (2009)

Quality of something. In serendipity research, as previously mentioned, embedded within the events described in Table 3.2 are often more specific descriptions of the qualities of the entities involved—the things encountered including the verbal, textual, or visual cues that trigger serendipity (McCay-Peet and Toms, 2015). Research often introduces serendipity as an event before focusing on these cues. The following section explores serendipity as a quality of something, the cues that prompt the experience of serendipity.

Various areas of computer science research (e.g., recommender systems, information retrieval) primarily approach serendipity as a quality of something, zeroing in on a specific problem to solve—namely improving user experience, reducing information overload, and bursting filter bubbles through the entities brought to users' attention (e.g., places, documents, photos, news stories). For example, Kotkov et al. (2016) pointed out that recommender system research carves off the "trigger" element of serendipity, defining a serendipitous item as relevant, novel and unexpected from the user perspective (Corneli et al., 2016).

Quality of "something" may be a social network (Jang, Choe, and Song, 2011) or digital environment (e.g., Renduchintala, Kelliher, and Sundaram, 2006). However, most prevalent is the quality of a recommendation or search result as serendipitous, reflecting the increasing amount of research on serendipity relating to recommender systems in the past few years. In general, this research is designed to test whether, for example, a mobile application, search engine, or recommender system facilitates serendipity. Zhang et al. (2012), for example, developed the Auralist, a music recommender, with the intent of balancing what they describe as conflicting goals of accuracy, diversity, novelty, and serendipity, to mimic what a friend or expert might recommend. Zhang et al. found that perceived serendipity is "usually, but not consistently, a positive contributor" (p. 21) to overall satisfaction, though this may be affected by factors external to the system (e.g., emotional state of the user). Zhang et al.'s findings contrast with findings by Ziegler et al. (2014) who found that serendipity and recommendation quality were negatively correlated. Ziegler et al. concluded that a better understanding of the "nature of serendipity" is needed moving forward to improve the quality of recommendations.

Table 3.3: Examples of research in which serendipity is approached as a quality of something

Quality of an Something	
Recommendations	
"serendipitous **music recommendations**"	Åman et al. (2014)
"serendipitous [**recommendation(s)**]"	Bordino et al. (2013b; 2014); Guy et al. (2015); Hornung et al. (2013); Rahman and Wilson (2015); Zhang et al. (2012)
"**perceived recommendation** serendipity"	Matt et al. (2014)
"serendipity of a place" [**recommendation**]	Hristova et al. (2016)
"serendipitous locations" [**recommendation**]	Kirman, Linehan, and Lawson (2012)
Search Results	
"Serendipitous **search result**"	André et al. (2009b); Bordino, Mejova, and Lalmas (2013a)
"Serendipitous **result[s]**"	Bordino, Mejova, and Lalmas (2013a); Rahman and Wilson (2015)
Social Networks	
"serendipitous **social networks**"	Jang, Choe, and Song (2011)
Digital environment	
Serendipitous as one of many "perceived **service characteristics**"	Liikkanen and Åman (2016)
"serendipitous **digital environment**"	McCay-Peet, Toms and Kelloway (2014; 2015)
"serendipitous design" of **user interfaces**; "serendipitous **search engine**"	Rahman and Wilson (2015)
"serendipitous **interfaces** that promote casual and chance encounters within a geographically distributed community"	Renduchintala, Kelliher, and Sundaram (2006)

Quality of someone. A growing body of research relates to serendipity as a quality of someone (Table 3.3). The quality of someone encompasses people's tendency to experience serendipity due to, for example, their personality traits or their behavior (either intentional or unintentional). Serendipity research relating to information behavior is much more common than research examining personality traits.

Only a handful of research has explored the personality traits of openness to experience and extraversion, for example, in relation to how frequently serendipity is experienced (e.g., Heinström, 2006; McCay-Peet, Toms, and Kelloway, 2015). While McCay-Peet at al. (2015) found no significant relationship between reported frequency of serendipity in digital information environments and openness to experience or extraversion, Heinström (2006) did find a significant relationship between extraversion and students' propensity to experience incidental information acquisition. More research is needed to understand how personality traits may influence serendipity as these too may inform what behaviors and frames of mind users may adopt to increase their opportunity for serendipity as desired.

Erdelez (1996, 1997, 1999) was among the first to explore what made some people more "serendipity-prone" (Merton and Barber, 2004) than others (see also Barber and Fox, 1958). Erdelez identified four types of information users who differ according to their perceptions of information encountering:

1. non-encounters,

2. occasional encounterers,

3. encounterers, and

4. super-encounters.

The four groups differ in the degree to which they encounter information, the extent that they can recall these encounters, their perception of the importance of information encounters, and their recognition of how their information encounters relate to their information behaviors. Super-encounters are of particular interest in the context of user strategies, as their behavior is worth emulating; a propensity to not only encounter information important to them but to encounter information that is important to family, friends, and colleagues (Erdelez, 1999). User strategies may involve, for example, the use of widely available sharing tools to share information encountered with friends, family, and colleagues (Erdelez and Rioux, 2000a, 2000b). Rather than relying solely on the digital environment to serve up serendipitous experiences, how can users gain control over their experience through their own online strategies and behaviors?

Serendipity is often framed as a behavior. Incidental exposure to online news, for example, related to incidental acquisition of information and information encountering, is referred to as a behavior (Yadamsuren and Erdelez, 2010). Because behaviors lead to serendipitous experiences, it is not surprising that serendipity has been characterized as a method, "a way of doing something" ("Method", n.d.) or behavior, "a way a person [...] acts or behaves" ("Behavior", n.d.). Seeking serendipity, trying to exert some control over a process, which is, by definition, unexpected, is a paradox (e.g., see McBirnie, 2008). However, even if aided through conscious behaviors or search strategies, research indicates that people may still perceive experiences as serendipitous (e.g., Martin and Quan-Haase, 2016; McCay-Peet and Toms, 2015). Frohlich, Wall, and Kiddle (2013) found there was a need to support "serendipitous browsing of photographs." So, rather than the emphasis on the photos, the things, the emphasis was on what behavior could be supported. Kirman et al.'s

(2012) GetLostBot issues challenges to users in the form of mysterious walking directions, which are only provided when the user has fallen into a routine. It has the potential to both make people aware of their behavior and possibly change it, encouraging people to explore more.

Table 3.4: Examples of research in which serendipity is approached as a quality of a behavior

Quality of someone	
The Individual	
Serendipity-prone; an individual's personality traits	Erdelez (1996; 1999); Heinström (2006); McCay-Peet, Toms, and Kelloway (2015)
Information Behavior	
"serendipitous **file exchange**"	Ahn and Pierce (2005)
"Serendipitous **social learning**"; Serendipitous, exploratory, and opportunistic are all grouped under umbrella "divergent **information behavior**"	Bilandzic, Schroeter, and Foth (2013)
"serendipitous search [...] occurs **when a user** with no a priori or totally unrelated intentions **interacts** with a system and acquires interesting information"	Bordino, Mejova, and Lalmas (2013a)
"serendipitous search **encounters**"	Bordino et al. (2013b)
Serendipitous browsing activities: "opportunistic **browsing**" and "involuntary **browsing**"	De Bruijn and Spence (2008)
"serendipitous **browsing** of photographs"	Frohlich, Wall, and Kiddle (2013)
"serendipitous news **exposure**"; "serendipitous news **discovery**"	Yadamsuren (2013)
"serendipitous news **exposure**"; "incidental **exposure** to online news"	Yadamsuren and Erdelez (2010)
"information **encountering**"	Erdelez (e.g., 2004)
"information **encountering**" "serendipitous information **discovery**"	Million et al. (2013)
"serendipitous **surfers**"	Gyllstrom and Moens (2012)

3.3   SUMMARY

Drivers of serendipity research play a large part in how serendipity is defined and approached across various fields of research and practice (e.g., human-computer interaction, interactive information retrieval, recommender systems, information science). A review of the research indicates that serendipity is approached as a process or experience and as a quality (of an event, something, or someone). However, a lack of systematic definitions of serendipity and related concepts in reports of research and a lack of consensus on definitions, have been noted (e.g., Kotkov et al., 2016); both shortfalls make it difficult to build theory. Moreover, inconsistencies exacerbated by the fact that the various disciplines and fields examining serendipity (e.g., information behavior, recommender systems) appear to be working in silos—odd considering the boundary-crossing often required to spark the very phenomenon under investigation.

CHAPTER 4

Facilitating Serendipity

4.1 INTRODUCTION

Serendipity is not a task; but as illustrated thus far, it is a by-product of performing other activities or tasks, and indeed could characterize the successful outcome of a task. One does not develop a *serendipity* application. While some (e.g. Van Andel, 1994) argue that one cannot engineer serendipity, others (e.g., Cunha, 2005; Campos and de Figueiredo, 2002) are not quite so definitive. We agree that one cannot "create serendipity" as to do so would render any output non-serendipitous, but we can create a fertile environment in which serendipity may flourish, and create specialized tools that may partially support the emergence of a serendipitous outcome (e.g., Leong et al, 2010; Liang, 2012).

In this chapter, we first examine how users engage with digital environments, and next examine how serendipity materializes within those environments. Finally, we examine the design issues and challenges that are needed to create serendipity-prone environments.

4.2 INTERACTION IN DIGITAL ENVIRONMENTS

As described in Chapter 1, a digital environment gives one a sense of place and purpose, enabling user interaction with a variety of information objects. This may be information search systems, collaborative work systems, social media, digital libraries, or any work task application. Virtually any interactive digital space provides opportunities for potentially serendipitous interactions (in much the same way that the physical world does).

The process of user interaction with a digital environment was described decades ago by Norman and Draper (1986): while engaged with an interactive system, a person formulates a *goal*, which is converted into an *intention* that is initiated by an *action* using an interface mechanism. Once the system responds, the user interprets and evaluates the *response* and compares it to the original *goal* before proceeding. This operates at the level of a single user-input/system-response. That is, it can be perceived at the level of typing a character to form a word and interpreting that character before the next character is typed. It can also be interpreted at a larger granular level. For example, a user needs to find a hotel, turns that goal into an intention to search the web, and enters the query into a search box; when the system responds, the user interprets and evaluates the result to ascertain whether the response meets the original goal. Many sequences of this cycle occur throughout any user-system interactive session (and often the user is in automatic processing, and unaware of each of these seemingly painstaking steps) (Figure 4.1).

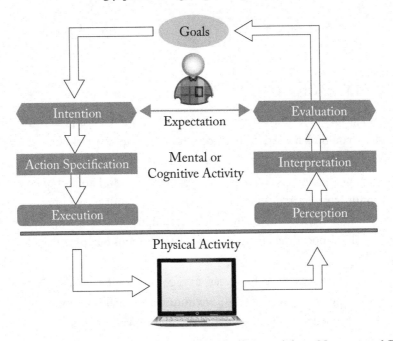

Figure 4.1: The interactive cycle of intentions to evaluation (adapted from Norman and Draper, 1986).

These sequences of interactivity occur in a two-dimensional space that varies in size by device (e.g., phone, tablet, desktop). That space becomes the user's window into a virtual world. Through that window, the user views and interacts with a rich tapestry of options that are implemented using primarily textual content, from menu options to bullets and paragraphs of text; visual cues represented by color, icons, and still or moving images; and sounds, from conversation to audio signals. Successful interaction in this space occurs when the system meets the user's mental model of that system, enabling a smooth communication between the two.

Given the limitations of a display, the user can only engage with that which is detectable (through visual or auditory cues), and can be understood or manipulated. The user needs to interpret the affordances of each object on that display, and additionally the textual affordances of each element of text. The challenge lies in the physical constraints of a display. Much like an iceberg with 90% of the mass underwater, almost any information system has a limited portion of its content visible at the "surface" (i.e., the interface) at any moment. Think of this with respect to Twitter, Google, GOV.UK, or even a "bank machine." Success for the user depends on how well the user can engage with a restricted set of visible objects to connect with those "below the surface."

Integral to this digital environment is the specific application that enables the task or work to be completed. This may be as mundane as word processing or as complex as a digital library, or a collaborative work system. This is analogically a task "layer" imposed on the system (although in reality it is more integrated than that). The range of possible actions becomes three-dimensional if one thinks of the elaborate data structure that interconnects the myriad of processes and objects. Only a small portion is ever visible to the user at a point in time, and that portion provides pathways and channels through the content of the system. For example, Google's sparse interface provides a single pathway (the search box) that interconnects with multiple other pathways (the results lists and filters). Somewhat similar, Twitter's and Instagram's hashtags provide a seemingly infinite number of interconnecting routes among content. But regardless of the task environment, the same user-input/system-response is the enabler of that interactivity, and the user can only view that which is visible at any moment in time.

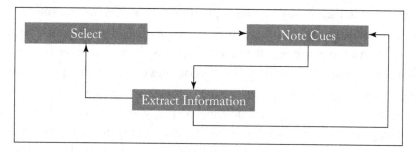

Figure 4.2: The Digital Instant that occurs many times over an interaction session (adapted from Toms, 1997).

When the user views this display in a specific task environment (e.g., Google, Twitter, a bank machine), the user needs to interpret the visible objects, deducing what each object and element of text (e.g., menu, titles) might mean. How the user proceeds will depend on the purpose of the interaction, from a targeted goal-focused task to a non-goal (or browse-based) mode, and whether this is a repetitive set of actions in a familiar environment or an infrequently used or novel system. But regardless of these issues, the user selects an object (eye gaze or formal mouse click), notes the cues emanating from the display which now act as an attention getting stimulus, and interprets and extracts any information bearing content to ascertain next steps. This digital instant (Toms 1997) occurs many times in the course of a session (see Figure 4.2). Sometimes these cues may be "landmarks" denoting position and place within system navigation, and sometimes these are textual affordances that the user interprets based on prior knowledge and experiences. Alternatively, the user may discount cues that are perceived as "window dressing" (e.g., advertisement, familiar website titles), and instead focus on those elements representing the actions the user wishes to take to satisfy that initial goal. This combined physical-virtual world is the one in which we need to enable serendipity to happen.

4.3   HOW SERENDIPITY HAPPENS IN DIGITAL ENVIRONMENTS

Given the explanation in the previous section, the user can only respond to cues present at the interface, and the system can only change those cues, based on what it knows or can predict about the user, or in response to some user action. It is at the point of those cues where the chance encounter with an anomaly or unexpected textual affordance is likely to occur. As illustrated in Figure 4.3, those cues serve as the *trigger*, enabling a novel observation. If the user acts on that cue, information encounter (Erdelez, 2000), or chance encounter (Toms, 2000b), then the cue may trigger an insight or curiosity and thus, the user may be on the pathway to a serendipitous finding. If the user ignores and discounts it, then it may be a lost opportunity. Once the user makes that observation, the user needs to process the cue, identifying any association or relationships; this may, in the digital environment, result in a faster response than the examples we have seen in science (see Chapter 1). That is, the incubation period may be short. The bisociation, a creative association between disparate pieces of information (Cunha, 2005; Koestler, 1964), may be computer-supported by specialized tools to aid the user in understanding the phenomenon (e.g., visualizations that juxtapose differing types of data), and the unexpected finding may be further computer-supported by showing the outcomes of the various bisociations as well as predicting a novel outcome. Ultimately, it will be the user who determines which outcome to act on, and it is at this point that we can describe something as merely problem solving or as serendipitous, something that resulted from that chance encounter with a trigger.

As described in Chapter 1, serendipity (as observed in science and engineering) tends to follow three patterns, and we argue that these patterns also occur in the digital environment (until a logical argument can be made to refute them). The application in a digital environment comes with some variations that pertain to the structure of that environment.

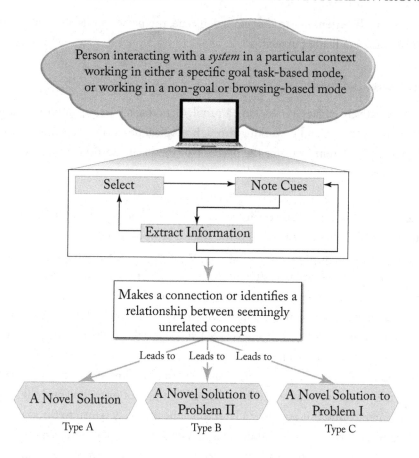

Figure 4.3: How the three types of serendipity unfold in a digital information environment.

Type A. From Observations to Solution

A person may be browsing the Web in an indiscriminate fashion from link to link, or reading and following the links in a newspaper, collecting bits of information as one progresses. The consumption of those bits of information leads to a novel discovery.

Type B. From Problem I to a Solution to Problem II

A person may be actively engaged in solving a problem, perhaps pursing an idea for a proposal or thesis, or planning a vacation. While following the usual leads, the person is presented with an unusual cue that triggers a change in focus that deviates from the planned and predicted pathway. The new pathway now may lead to new information about a different project, or perhaps a recipe for dinner. In this case that anomalous chance encounter which appears totally out of character leads to a surprise finding. By attending to the anomalous cue, the person finds a solution to something that was not the problem being pursued.

Type C. Unexpected Solutions

A person may be actively engaged in solving a problem, perhaps pursing an idea for a proposal or thesis, or planning a vacation and is working through a logical process when exposure to something unexpected triggers a different focus for the proposal or thesis, or vacation, none of which had been previously entertained.

Unlike the examples discussed earlier in Chapter 1, in the case of digital environments, the key facilitator (other than human sagacity) is the system (a word used in this chapter to refer to any piece of technology or application), and what/how it presents to the user. As illustrated in Figure 4.3, a user interacts with a system using the interface tools and the dynamic content supplied. In the case of Type A, the user has no purpose, but in Types B and C, the user has a core issue to resolve. In all three types, the user notes an element of the display, which serves as the trigger, causing the user to pause and consider it; this cue is unexpected and anomalous. The user may follow-up immediately and fully understand the value, or the user may store this new information for later digestion, which allows the cue to percolate until fully understood. At some point, the user will make the connection — the "ah ha" moment—the bisociation. If it occurs instantaneously, it may influence immediate user interactions; if it occurs at a later time, the user may return to the system or another system, or recognize the connection external to any system. Once it has occurred than the next step is the manipulation or modification of that connection to formulate a novel serendipitous solution.

4.4   DESIGN ISSUES AND REQUIREMENTS

Within user-system interaction in a digital environment, the conditions identified in Chapter 1 still hold.

1. There will be an observation of some visual (or auditory) stimuli that is unanticipated and anomalous;

2. The user must have the human cognitive capability and knowledge to recognize the anomalous state; and, additionally,

3. The mental space at that time to absorb it.

4. The incubation and consumption time required to "connect the dots" may be almost instantaneous occurring within a single user session, or it may take time and tenacity external to the system for the user to process.

5. There will be a significant outcome that also may occur external to the system.

Clearly, until humans have bionic inserts or some form of digital augmentation that enhance human capability, conditions (b) and (c) are outside system capabilities. The system does not know what the user is thinking, and is still unable to know precisely what experiences a user has had since the last interaction with the system. Paradoxically, the system is quite limited, having only the capability to respond to what it knows about the human or respond to human input, although the system may influence and stimulate the human. Much has been written about creativity and the creative process as well as how people create meaning or interpret the elements of a situation. Where the system stops and the human starts is a grey area. What goes on inside the human head and simple human capabilities and limitations are outside the scope of this book. Thus, the system is the supporting actor, the apprentice and personal assistant, albeit a very smart one, in this process.

Instead, the more productive approach is in facilitating the other three conditions as functional requirements of any system for which serendipitous outcomes are considered an advantage:

1. enabling the "anomaly" or the chance encounter to trigger an event; this is indeed what most of the solutions discussed in the next section have strived to achieve;

2. supporting the user in "connecting the dots," that is, identifying the relationship between the cue and what is percolating inside the user's head, or showing relationships between the cue and other incongruent elements; and

3. supporting the user in reaching a significant surprise outcome; this also has been rarely if ever attempted.

Thus, these become the functions required for computer support of human activities that may lead to serendipitous outcomes. These are not simple for systems that run on logic and rules that converge on a solution to develop. However, a computer can run through many variations abiding loosely by human rules to emerge with unimaginable possibilities for the human subsequently to consider.

4.5   OPERATIONALIZING THOSE DESIGN CONSIDERATIONS

To date, we have no set of systematic requirements for achieving a system that facilitates serendipity. Any system that supports serendipity must be able to facilitate those three functions identified in the last section. But the challenge is in how to operationally achieve any of them.

Van Andel (1994) identified 17 patterns (e.g., analogy, successful error, playing) from his analysis of over 1,000 serendipitous outcomes, which may be, given the date of publication, safely described as outcomes facilitated by non-digital information environments. Some such as analogy may be semi-automated in a digital environment, while others are simply descriptive. Toms

(2000a) proposed four techniques to support serendipity after observing around 50 participants in a multi-session study of digital news reading. Björneborn (2010), who observed library users, identified ten dimensions of library spaces such as diversity, contrast and imperfection that may have the potential to enable divergent behavior. Most developments to date have focused on enabling a chance encounter, but few have defined a prescription for how to achieve it (André et al., 2009a).

We examined the techniques that have either been proposed to date, or have been developed and or tested in various research projects to identify likely techniques to support the three functions. At this point, we do not have any solutions that have been demonstrated as successful in the real world. Potential solutions to support the three functions are described below.

1. Enables anomalies and incongruities

Description: Enabling chance (which may be initially construed as "blind luck" or a happy accident) is elemental to serendipity. Chance in this context means something that is uncharacteristic or odd compared to the activity currently in focus; something in the current display is perceived as not fitting the normal pattern expected at that point in the interaction, and that something has the potential to become a trigger.

Requirement: The display must provide an element that is not what the user expects, and thus is seemingly unrelated to what the user is currently doing or focused on. There is a caveat to implementing this: a deliberate attempt to engage the user in examining such an element means that the system also needs to draw the user's attention to what at surface value seems irrelevant. In the web environment in particular, a user may have "blinker blindness" or functional fixity such that visual cues intended to grab attention are ignored. This is not unlike the scientists who seemed initially unaware of a solution that when examined in hindsight seemed so obvious (Shapiro, 1986).

The anomalous element may be an item in a list, a text box, audio signal, or image of some sort. The challenge will be in the semantic distance between what the system normally expects to display, and the serendipitous trigger, and in how the system "knows" what the element of focus is, as well as its attributes. Critical is how the user's attention is acquired and whether the user is receptive to a "seducible moment" (Spool, 2002).

Enabling this aspect has been attempted in a number of ways.

- **Randomness:** Shuffle listening to music (e.g., Leong, Vetere, and Howard, 2006) or random viewing of photos (Leong, Harper, and Regan, 2011) when the random selection is unconstrained with no filters. In case of music or photos, the entire collection had the potential to be selected. Liang (2012) argues that the system needs to have some form of "unexpectedness generating" that is created by uncertainty as related to information, and attention.

- **Unexpected:** In weighting items to display in a recommender system for Netflix, Lu et al. (2012) assigned higher weights to items in the tail than to those identified as the most popular.

- **Dissimilarity, i.e., semantically distant:** Laquinta et al. (2008) created a recommender that proposes items whose descriptions were semantically distant from the user profiles; similarly, Zhang et al.(2012) presented items that were dissimilar to the ones previously listened to.

- **Diversification:** Both Adamopoulos and Tuzhilin (2014) and Ziegler et al. (2005) maximized the sematic variation in a results/recommendation list.

- **Quantity of information presented:** de Bruijn and Spence (2001) proposed increasing the amount of information in a display such as scrolling news-bars, headlines, stock prices.

- **Anomalous Result:** Toms (2000b) implemented a tool intended to produce a set of articles that were very much like the article that was currently being displayed. The weighted Boolean algorithm for making the match often displayed articles that lacked any similarity at all which provided anomalous but novel results. The concept was reproduced in a second study (Toms and McCay-Peet, 2009) which returned the first paragraph of the displayed article as query in wikiSearch, which also provided unusual and diverse results.

2. Identifies the relationships—the connections and bisociations—among different concepts
Description: Enabling a comparison of concepts in which one is clearly well understood by the user while the other may not be is a pivotal point on the pathway to serendipity. Furthermore, the defining of novel relationships between disparate entities is a core indicator of creativity (Boden, 1996; Ford, 1999; Koestler, 1964).

Requirement: In the previous function, the role of the system was to focus the attention of the user as a starting point. In this function, the intent is to show the relationships among concepts, which may fit any of these patterns:

1. a concept that is currently being cognitively processed by the user with another concept that is present on, or suggested by, what is present on the display;

2. two concepts that are being probed by the user who does not fully understand the relationship among them: or,

3. two concepts that have unexpectedly emerged on the display due to some prior action of the user.

In the case of (1), the system needs to understand what the user is working on/thinking, which may be managed through some form of personalization, or predictive actions based on historic actions, on a direct input from the user. In the case of (2) and (3), it is about presenting why those concepts have a relationship. In some cases, the concepts as presented might simply pique the user's curiosity, while in others, the system can assist in aiding the user in that understanding (not unlike what one would expect from a good assisted learning system). Note that simple web links may, but do not necessarily, enable this opportunity; this is not about precision, recall, accuracy, high rating, satisfaction and so on. While an element of, for example, similarity is important, the interconnections among the concepts may be for many different reasons including dissimilarity, novelty, user, and/or community rating.

Enabling this aspect has been attempted in a number of ways.

- **Interdisciplinary cross fertilization** at the interface to two disciplines is known to be a pertinent site for the proliferation of new ideas (Foster and Ford, 2003).

- **Indirect associations:** Swanson (1986) identified the connection between Raynaud's disease and fish oil by observing that both appeared frequently in article titles that included blood viscosity, platelet aggregation and vascular reactivity. This semi-automated approach has been refined by multiple projects (Swanson and Smalheiser, 1997; Lindsay and Gordon 1999; Gordon and Dumais 1998; Weeber et al. 2001; Yetisgen-Yildiz, 2006) to represent the underlying structure that represents this algorithm: if a is related to b and if c is related to b, then there must be some sort of connection between a and c.

- **Co-author networks:** in creating scholarly paper recommenders, Sugiyama and Kan (2015) created co-author networks with an emphasis on the co-authors' papers rather than those of the primary authors.

- **Collaborative filtering:** provision of content based on the action of others such that the differences between two people (based on profiles) become the source for novelty and anomaly.

- **Laterality:** Campos and de Figuerido (2002) developed elements of lateral thinking (de Bono, 1970) in Max, an intelligent agent that navigates the Web on the user's behalf. Max (a) generated alternatives by selecting concepts from random profiles, (b) selected both highly relevant and less relevant items using exponential probabilistic distribution, and (c) substituted some concepts with related concepts, and thus presents the user with novel suggestions based on these multiple decisions, and a heuristic evaluation that also includes the user's profile.

- **Visualization:** Saleem et al. (2013) enabled association among large sets of linked data so that relationships that are not immediately obvious among concepts may be explored.

3. Identifies potential outcomes given a set of bisociations

Description: Enabling a novel, unexpected outcome is a challenging task. Given that the user's attention has been engaged, and that the connection has been made, the system now needs to aid the user in reaching that game-changing surprising conclusion. What does that odd item, anomaly, or incongruous connection actually mean? As Boden (1990a) notes: "a merely novel idea is one which can be described and/or produced by the same set of generative rules as are other, familiar ideas. A genuinely original, or creative, ideas is one which cannot" (p. 78).

Requirement: In the previous functions, the user noted the trigger, and identified a relationship among elements even though the user may not yet recognize the full value of that association. This third function now aids the user in exploring what this relationship might mean, and how it can be used. We know of no one who has induced a serendipitous outcome in digital environments. We have multiple options for developing cues to serve as triggers, and ways of looking at relationships among concepts differently. But arguable, we cannot definitively say that we have put all of this together to create a serendipitous digital information environment—*yet*! Instead, we can look to the creative problem solving research for ideas as well as those proposed with respect to serendipity. Some of the techniques include the following.

- **Reasoning by analogy:** compare a problem with something that has little or nothing to do with the one at hand (Bawden, 1986; Toms, 2000a; Van Andel, 1994).

- **Identify** the connection that may integrate a set of discrete entities (Bawden, 1986; Ford, 1999).

- **Identify the pattern** among a set of concepts (Ford, 1999), which may be semantic, structural, linguistic, by color, by size, etc.

- **Brainstorming** to produce a list of possibilities aided by a useful intelligent agent who can make pertinent suggestions and additionally evaluate options.

- **Reversal:** looking at things from the opposite direction.

- **Exaggeration:** consider variable outside the normal range.

- **Distortion:** distort normal relationships between variables; and

• **Wishful thinking:** fantasy—imagine if…

4. Integrate with the user application

Description: This was not identified as a function of serendipity, but is integral to enabling serendipity in other applications. To be usable, the serendipity functionality needs to be seamlessly integrated within the application's task-based functionality.

Requirement: Integrating serendipity in other applications is not analogical to integrating the function of cut and paste from application to application. It is not like inserting a dictionary, or an "I am lucky" filter or even as has been suggested a "serendipity button" which has appeared in multiple locations on the web (the origin of which is unknown). Clearly from all that has been written, the openness of a system to maximize the cues available to the user and enhance the user's ability to explore via multiple pathways is the critical component. This also means judiciously enabling the requirement of systems to ensure the user is in control—one of Shneiderman's "eight golden rules" (Shneiderman et al., 2016). For example, Toms (1997) provided a slider which enabled the user to control how precise the relevance would be, while Benjamin et al. (2014) provided a creativity slider that went from "select" the object to "wild." Implementing the serendipity functionality with strong visual cues to engage the attention of the user from simple presentation to views of large data/information sets dominates many initiatives (see, for example, Thudt et al., 2012).

While we could not find solid evidence for applications that enabled all functions, there have been some promising implementations.

• *Contact Space* (Jeffery and McGrath, 2000) and *Serendipity* (Eagle and Pentland, 2005) are collaborative virtual environments that were intended to support online chance encounters.

• *Bohemian Bookshelf* (Thudt et al., 2012) contained five interlinked visualizations of a book collections that enabled: multiple visual access points and multiple pathways through the collection based on different attributes of books, and showed relationships among the books based on those same attributes. The application identified novel visual representation of the collection enabling interaction with the collection that was engaging and playful.

• *Twitter* has emerged in many studies (see, for example, Kop, 2012; Quan-Haase, Martin, and McCay-Peet, 2015) as a fertile environment to facilitate serendipity, although that was not its intended purpose. More research is needed to deconstruct that environment to ascertain what makes it so. Is it, for example, the user control on followers, the cross fertilization by the juxtapositioning of hashtags, and retweets, or the presentation of diverse content?

4.6   SUMMARY

As evident from the attempts to date, facilitating serendipity and nurturing an environment in which serendipity may happen is not straightforward. Causing serendipity to occur is an even greater, if not impossible, challenge, although the promise of artificial intelligence and its successors may have an effective solution. In our systematic examination of the prior research and development, we found very few examples of a development that supported all three core functions (i.e., enables anomalies, supports connects, support for reaching a surprise outcome) required to enable serendipity. Many developments have tested various approaches to enabling a chance encounter with a trigger or in displaying connections and potential relationships among concepts and objects.

While many claims are made about a tool or feature being serendipitous, those claims can be challenged (i.e., merely saying it is serendipitous which often means a surprise does not make it serendipitous), and have yet to be validated.

The bigger challenge in digital environments is in how to integrate such functionality into existing applications, that is, those everyday tools that users use on a regular basis. The existing functionality that enables a user to converge on a solution to a problem, works against the divergence that is needed to enable serendipity. Pathways and navigation channels are outside the individual's control, limited by the algorithms that may restrict the display, and as discussed in Chapter 2, may create filter bubbles (Pariser, 2011). What we need is what Zetter (2011) calls a "balanced information diet," one that challenges us, provides other points of view, and sometimes simply makes us uncomfortable.

CHAPTER 5

Methods and Measurement

I do not know whether serendipity is a phenomenon that occurs with sufficient frequency, whether it is capable of being observed with sufficient accuracy, and whether it is sufficiently controllable to lead to useful research into its nature. At least, it is an inspiring phenomenon and a very interesting subject for "pure" research (Bernier, 1960, p. 277).

Given the diversity of the elements contained in serendipity research, serendipity research designs deploy a potpourri of research methods from interviews to experiments, which generate a diverse set of both qualitative and quantitative data for analyzes. Selecting the best methods to understand aspects of serendipity or tools to support serendipity is a challenge; "serendipity is by definition not particularly susceptible to systematic control and prediction" (Foster and Ford, 2003, p. 337). Bernier's (1960) reservations about the application of research methods to observe and control serendipity continue to ring true almost 60 years later. Serendipity is quite simply very difficult to study (e.g., Erdelez, 2004; Kotkov et al., 2016; McBirnie, 2008; Rahman and Wilson, 2015).

As discussed in Chapter 2, the impetus to understand the phenomena now extends beyond pure research into development for real world application. Thus, research designs are much more diverse and extensive than those used in researching typical social science phenomena. Through a diversity of method, research motivation, topic, context and measurement this chapter provides an overview of some of the current serendipity research methods.

5.1 RESEARCH DESIGN

As with any research project, the research design depends on the purpose of the research, which in turn determines the selection of data collecting methods, techniques for analysis, and the measures to use. In serendipity research, the designs have tended to be:

- descriptive studies (e.g., Makri and Blandford, 2012; McCay-Peet and Toms, 2015);

- correlational studies to examine the relationships among variables (e.g., Heinström, 2006; McCay-Peet, Kelloway, and Toms, 2015); or

- experimental (e.g., Taramigkou, Apostolou, and Mentza, 2017; Thudt, Hinrichs, and Carpendale, 2012; Toms, 2000b).

Within these various designs, one or more methods have been deployed. Based on prior research to date (as described in the previous chapters), we have grouped broadly the purposes that have emerged from our systematic review of serendipity research with the methods and analyzes that have been used to date (see Table 5.1). We refer the reader to the many textbooks about research design, methods and data analysis for a generic explanation of how and when to use them. In this chapter, we describe how some of the methods have been deployed in serendipity research. Evident from these summary descriptions is the number of multiple methods, or mixed methods research studies. Some methods such as observation have primarily been used in the physical environment (see, for example, Björneborn, 2008) and are not examined here. At the end of this chapter we address the measurement problem in the very quantitative sense of that word.

Table 5.1: Methods and analyzes used in serendipity research

	Purpose	Method
1	Understand the phenomena	Interview, focus group, diary
2	Understand human perception of the phenomena	Interview, focus group, diary, questionnaires
3	Understand human individual differences with respect to the phenomena	Questionnaires
4	Understand what facilitates the phenomena	Interview, focus group, diary, questionnaires
5	Deconstruct the phenomena to extract its core processes and influential elements	Interview, focus group, diary
6	Develop and test cues to trigger the phenomena	Logfiles, verbal protocols,
7	Develop and test techniques to facilitate connections and relationships that have the potential to enable the phenomena	Logfiles, questionnaires, verbal protocols
8	Develop and test techniques to facilitate a serendipitous interpretation of the connections, i.e., get to the valuable outcome	Logfiles, questionnaires, verbal protocols
9	Assess an outcome as serendipitous	Diaries, interviews, existing documents, questionnaires

5.2   INTERVIEWS

Background

Interviews are organized, purposeful conversations between researchers and participants that may take place face-to-face or via email, telephone, or over the internet using a software application and may be structured (similar to survey questionnaires), semi-structured, or unstructured. There are three core elements of an interview as a method for collecting data:

1. they take place between two people;

2. the researcher and participant have different roles in the conversation; and

3. there is a clear purpose to the interview (Luo and Wildemuth, 2009).

Interviews result in piles of textual data, and thus measurement in this context like any qualitative data set does not fit the norm of what is typically considered "measurement." This is very much about understanding, which is achieved through various types of qualitative analyzes such as thematic analysis, and content analysis.

Use in Serendipity Research

Interviews are invaluable for answering the *how* and *why* questions related to serendipity. Thus, the primary reasons interviews are employed in serendipity research are to achieve four purposes from Table 5.1, namely:

1. understand the phenomena,

2. understand human perception of the phenomena,

3. understand human individual differences with respect to the phenomena, and

9. assess an outcome as serendipitous.

While sometimes used as the sole method of data collection in serendipity studies (Barber and Fox, 1958; McBirnie, 2008; McCay-Peet and Toms, 2015), interviews are often used in conjunction with other methods such as diaries (Leong et al., 2010), naturalistic observation and think-aloud protocols (Björneborn, 2008), and experiments that involve the collection of log data and relevance judgments (André et al., 2009b).

Although not always explicitly described as such in research reports, semi-structured interviews appear to be the most extensively used interview approach in serendipity research (e.g., Bellotti et al., 2008; Martin and Quan-Haase, 2016; McBirnie, 2008; McCay-Peet and Toms, 2015). Serendipity is a complex phenomenon and semi-structured interviews allow researchers to examine specific aspects of serendipity of interest but also give researchers the flexibility to explore related and perhaps unexpected aspects that emerge during interviews. As part of a series of studies, Bellotti et al. (2008) used the semi-structured interview approach with 32 participants to understand leisure and information behavior relating to leisure and to help evaluate the concept of a tool that supports serendipity, a mobile leisure guide. McBirnie (2008) used semi-structured interview techniques to interview two jazz improvisers and eight academics to understand serendipity and the conditions that may facilitate it. In this section, we focus on one study (Martin and Quan-Haase, 2016), which employed semi-structured interviews in which the motivation for research was one of the previously identified main drivers of serendipity research (Chapter 2): physical vs. digital environments.

Example

Martin and Quan-Haase (2016) applied the semi-structured interview approach to gain an understanding of serendipity in the historical research process and further found the method useful for identifying how serendipity may be supported through digital and physical environments, and, like McBirnie (2008), through training.

Through in-depth, semi-structured interviews with 20 historians, using grounded theory methods, Martin and Quan-Haase (2016) investigated "the changing research practices of historians," contrasting "their experiences of serendipity in physical and digital environments" (p. 1008). To start, ten participants were interviewed and data analyzed before modifications to interview questions were made and ten more participants were interviewed using the constant comparative method (Glaser and Strauss, 1967). Interviews were selected over diary studies and observation in order to gain more detailed accounts and allow the authors to ask probing questions (Martin and Quan-Haase, 2016). However, the authors also note that their selected method made it difficult to recruit participants because of the need for the interviews to take place in-person. Despite the challenge, the method allowed them to identify themes that serve to increase our understanding of serendipity and highlight the ways in which the movement from physical to digital environments has affected historians. They found that historians perceived themselves as active agents in their experience of serendipity, doing things like browsing created opportunities for serendipity. Another key finding included the identification of the need to help historians make connections between physical and digital resources by better integrating these types of resources; to this end, primary source context and organizational context (e.g., library stacks) should be supported through digital tools. What was evident from this paper was that semi-structured interviews helped provide a deeper understanding of how historians viewed the shift from physical to digital and how serendipity, and the historical research process in general, could be supported through thoughtful design of digital environments.

5.3   DIARIES

Background

Diaries are another way that researchers can capture and observe the thoughts and behaviors of participants. Rather than a computer system or the researcher capturing participant data, however, in the case of research diaries, it is the participant who actively captures their own data by recording their experiences, thoughts, and feelings over time. The diaries are solicited by the researcher and they are essentially self-report logs that may be written records or include images and other objects that contextualize the participants' experiences. Like interviews, diaries may be unstructured, structured or semi-structured, each providing different levels of guidance to the participant on what should be recorded in the diary and when. Diaries may be comprised of pen and paper, but more commonly researchers are using other methods such as web-based diaries (Shelbe and Wildemuth, 2009).

Diaries may result in both open-ended textual responses and items that can be quantified in some way. Like interviews and focus groups, this is very much about *understanding*, which is achieved through various types of qualitative analyzes such as thematic analysis and content analysis. But structured diaries also create categorical data or data that may classified in some way such that the items can be coded and thus counted in some way to show frequencies or magnitude of a set of elements, events or processes, and or the relationships and correlations among them.

Use in Serendipity Research

Diaries, like interviews and focus groups, are employed in serendipity research to achieve four purposes from Table 5.1, namely:

1. understand the phenomena,

2. understand human perception of the phenomena,

3. understand human individual differences with respect to the phenomena, and

9. assess an outcome as serendipitous.

The diary method has been used many times in serendipity research (e.g., Bentley, Basapur and Chowdhury, 2011; Leong et al., 2010; Rahman and Wilson, 2015; Sun et al., 2011; Williamson, 1998). Williamson (1998) asked participants to keep telephone diaries indicating the intent of their phone call and what was discussed in order to understand the information behaviors of older adults. Through this method and combined with interviews, Williams found that participants encountered information when they were not explicitly looking for it, often through interactions with other people. While Sawaizumi et al. (2009) used diaries as a method of data collection, they were also interested in diaries as a means to support serendipity. Participants were given "serendipity cards," paper-based cards, to fill in over a period of a few months. The cards prompted participants to fill in information on observations that they made as well as their hypothesis, the who, what, when, where, why, and how, and the result. The intent was to nurture observations in the incubation period of serendipity and encourage deeper thinking that could potentially lead to a serendipitous outcome. No incidences of serendipity, however, were captured in Sawaizumi et al.'s study, highlighting the difficulty of capturing a phenomenon that for many is infrequent and intermittent. As these examples (Sawaizumi et al., 2009; Williamson, 1998) illustrate, the rationale for conducting diary studies is similar to that of using interview methods: to gain a greater understanding of the phenomenon, how it may be facilitated, and how well a tool supports serendipity within a particular context. The remainder of this section focuses on research by Leong et al. (2010) that used the diary method to understand serendipity as user experience in the context of music listening.

Example

Through interpretivist qualitative research, Leong et al. (2010) examined people's experiences of serendipity while listening to music. To do this, they argued it was necessary to capture this in the field, in the natural setting of people's lives where serendipity happens. A diary was given to each participant in which they were instructed to record their listening experiences for seven weeks. Because participants were asked to record their experiences in any way they chose in the diary, the quality of expression was uneven, ranging from "perfunctory" to "vivid" (p. 258). And while Leong et al. (2010) note the many insights gained through an analysis of the diaries, they also note their fragmentary nature and the need to conduct open-ended interviews "to 'thicken' these descriptions, and get closer to the whole person and the weight of the experience as lived and felt" (p. 260). The diaries, however, were further used in face-to-face interviews to help explore the stories recorded, to help fill in some of the blanks, and create shared understanding. So while participants recorded serendipitous experiences in their diaries, these experiences were explored further to help understand further details surrounding the experience. Leong et al. (2010) found "that at the heart of the experience of serendipity was the emergence of powerful personal meanings out of seemingly random coincidence of events" (p. 263). In relation to methods, they conclude:

> The methods we used and the kind of insights into serendipity they offered, do not allow us to measure or compare the intensity of serendipitous experiences, nor do they allow us on the basis of such comparison to argue that one form of digital shuffle might be more effective than another. What our account offers instead is an understanding of how to shape the processes that need to come together in order for a serendipitous experience to emerge (p. 263).

While the diary study method used by Leong et al. (2010) may not be the go-to method for comparing, for example, how well one digital musical listening tool supports serendipity over another, this method does inform what conditions need to be in place for serendipity to happen.

5.4   EXISTING DOCUMENTS

Background

Existing documents may include almost any form of textual artifact. These sources tend to have been written without any intention of examining serendipity as the purpose for their creation. They may be published or unpublished, take a formal or informal form, and may be physical or digital. Official documents, memos, and diaries are all potential sources for data. This source of data is unobtrusive at least with respect to the current study, as their collection by the researcher had no impact on the original participants; the documents are natural in the sense that they were not created within the confines of the research study (Wildemuth, 2009b).

Use in Serendipity Research

Because existing documents are records of the past, they achieve three purposes from Table 5.1, namely to:

1. understand the phenomena,

4. understand what facilitates the phenomena, and

9. assess an outcome as serendipitous.

Using existing documents is to date an uncommon source in serendipity research, although the few studies have isolated many incidences of serendipity that have not necessarily been described as such by its authors. Campanario (1996) first used this method to understand the phenomenon of serendipity in science. He analyzed 205 Citation Classics Database, commentaries by the authors of 400 of the most highly cited scientific papers together with the original papers to uncover whether and how serendipity may have played a role in the discoveries. These commentaries were classified using Van Andel's (1994) 17 proposed serendipity patterns or "ways in which unsought findings have been made" (Van Andel's, 1994, p. 640). More recently, Erdelez and Beheshti (see Erdelez et al., 2016), used informetric analysis to examine serendipity research output in multiple disciplines and found that different disciplines have developed different terminology relating to serendipity and that serendipity research often exists in silos with few connections between serendipity researchers across different fields. This method, therefore, appears to be an interesting way to understand the growing field of serendipity research itself and see differences in approaches and gaps in connections among pockets of research in the area.

Using existing documents, thus, results in quantities of qualitative data from the contents of those documents, which may be analyzed using thematic and content analyzes. But additionally the metadata from those documents may be used to describe the elements and their relationships and thus used to describe serendipity research output. The example described below (Rubin, Burkell, and Quan-Haase, 2011) provides an illustration of the use of the existing documents in serendipity research.

Example

Through a systematic search of GoogleBlog, Rubin et al. (2011) conducted an analysis of 56 blog posts that described "naturally occurring accounts of chance encounters" (n.p.). Grounded theory was used to analyze the data. While Rubin et al. did not restrict where these chance encounters took place—physical or digital—they found that 24 took place in a digital information environment. Through the analysis they identified four main facets relating to *the find*—prepared mind, act of noticing, chance, and fortuitous outcome (see also Table 3.1), which both helps to explain the phenomenon in the context of everyday life and points to how it may be facilitated by digital information environments. Rubin et al. note, for example, that particular attention should be paid to creating digital information environments that enhance the facets of noticing and the prepared mind. While the advantage of the existing document approach is that the accounts are realistic and self-generated rather than obtained through artificial means, a drawback is that "these texts do not address all of the nuances of a chance encounter episode" (Rubin et al., 2011, n.p.). A large sample of accounts, however, may lessen such concerns.

5.5   VERBAL PROTOCOLS

Background

Verbal protocols are used to collect information on the cognitive processes of participants by encouraging the vocalized explanation of actions, either during (think aloud), or immediately after (talk after), interacting with a system. Think-aloud protocols may be performed concurrently during a task or retrospectively. While the concurrent think-aloud happens in real-time, retrospective think-aloud protocols allow the participant to complete their tasks naturally before being asked to relive and describe their thoughts. Verbal protocols are usually used together with screen capture that records in a video the actions of the user and response of the system. In think-aloud protocols, the video and/or audio record simultaneously and overlay the screen capture. In the case of talk after (i.e., retrospective protocols), the recording replayed after the session is finished to prompt participants for explanations of actions and thoughts during their task. There are limitations to both types: talk aloud requires participants to multi-task, that is, to explain what they are doing currently while solving another problem or doing another task which may slow and interfere with task performance and impact data collected; talk after may lead participants to blend other memories leading to misleading data (Oh and Wildemuth, 2009; Van den Haak et al., 2004).

The data from verbal protocols form *streams of consciousness* whose value is in the context in which the actions occurred. Toms (1997) mapped the comments made in talk-after session to logfiles (see Section 5.7), which enabled coding and content analysis of the comments according to point in the process, and further examination of the process in a quantitative way. The value to serendipity research was in identifying the surprise find—the trigger, the participant's explanation of the connection, and the value of that connection to the participant.

Use in Serendipity Research

Verbal protocols are actively used in research in the digital information environment as they enable greater understanding of user actions and thus tend to be used for the following purposes in serendipity research as identified in Table 5.1:

4. understand what facilitates the phenomena,

5. deconstruct the phenomena to extract its core processes and influential elements,

6. develop and test cues to trigger the phenomena,

7. develop and test techniques to facilitate connections and relationships that have the potential to enable the phenomena, and

8. develop and test techniques to facilitate a serendipitous interpretation of the connections, i.e., get to the valuable outcome.

Verbal protocols, as previously noted in this chapter, have been used in serendipity research in combination with screen capture and logfile analysis to provide a rich data set in which the user actions and behaviors are objectively recorded and supplemented by cognitive thought processes for an understanding of the reasons behind those behaviors. Björneborn (2008), Yadamsuren and Erdelez (2010), and Toms (1997) used verbal protocols in order to link participants' thoughts directly to the observed information encountering and divergent behaviors. While verbal protocols are useful for evaluating the effectiveness of a system to support chance encounters (Toms, 1997), they are also useful for gaining an understanding of how people experience information encounters (Björneborn, 2008).

Example

To "understand whether and how a particular digital information environment creates opportunities for serendipity" (p. 9) Makri et al. (2015) used think aloud with screen capture to collect the actions and behaviors of 45 participants interacting with different types of information environments in a controlled setting. Solomon and Bronstein (2016) note the difficulty in directly observing serendipity and thus the verbal protocols + screen capture provide a good compromise.

Makri et al. took a naturalistic approach by asking participants to perform information tasks of their own choosing which led to a variety of tasks including, for example, browsing news sites and looking for a specific product to purchase. Participants—computer science students—were divided into three groups with participants in each group asked to use one of three types of digital information environment: news sites, digital libraries, and e-commerce sites. Participants were not aware that the focus of the study was serendipity and a post-task questionnaire revealed that most were not familiar with the phenomenon. Participants were asked to think-aloud during the tasks, allowing the researchers to capture participants' verbalization of what they were doing and why. A recording was made of the screen as well as an audio recording. A follow-up interview was conducted to probe instances that were noted as both useful and unexpected and understand. Using inductive and deductive analysis, both observational and interview data was coded. While Makri et al. note that due to the unexpectedness of serendipity it is "difficult to observe in controlled research environment" (p. 10), with careful research design it is possible and such an approach enables researchers to evaluate how well digital environments support serendipity. Through the study, they found instances in which participants found "useful information unexpectedly when not looking for anything in particular and finding useful information unexpectedly when looking for information on something else" (p. 5). Makri et al. argue that the direct observation approach allows for a better understanding of the types of interactions that support serendipity, which is imperative to understanding the requirements of serendipitous digital information environments.

5.6   QUESTIONAIRES

Background
Questionnaires allow researchers to collect a range of data relating to participant perceptions, attributes, opinions and behaviors through closed and open-ended questions and scalar responses to statements (Hank, Jordan, and Wildemuth, 2009). Questionnaires generate a lot of quantitative data. The analyzes depending on the design can be as straightforward as counts, frequencies, and percentages, and thus very descriptive of the phenomena, to comparative, correlational, and even experimental analyzes that test differences among the variables.

Use in Serendipity Research
Questionnaires are invaluable for answering the how and why questions related to serendipity. Thus, the primary reasons interviews are employed in serendipity research are to achieve four purposes from Table 5.1, namely:

1. understand the phenomena,

2. understand human perception of the phenomena,

3. understand human individual differences with respect to the phenomena, and

9. assess an outcome as serendipitous.

Questionnaires have been used extensively in serendipity research (e.g., Guy et al., 2015; Hornung et al., 2013; McCay-Peet, Toms, and Kelloway, 2015; Million et al., 2013) for multiple purposes. Some research projects (e.g., Yadamsuren and Erdelez, 2010; 2016) have used questionnaires as a screening technique to select participants who appear to have more of a propensity of information encountering for participation in further research. This technique allows for richer interview data to be collected as it ensures interviewed participants will have something to say about an aspect of serendipity or related concepts like information encountering. In order to better understand the psychological aspects of incidental information acquisition (IIA), Heinström (2006) used a series of established scales for measuring personality and approaches to studying as well as statements relating feelings, information seeking styles, and propensity for IAA on Likert scales. Questionnaires have also been used post-experiment as a way to gather information regarding serendipitous experiences with systems (e.g., Taramigkou et al., 2017; Toms, 1997; Toms and McCay-Peet, 2009). Relative to the qualities of recommendations and search results, questionnaires have been used to collect data on users' perceptions of content or information including, for example, how unknown yet valuable (Campos and Figueiredo, 2002), not relevant but interesting (André et al., 2009b), interesting (Toms, 1997), or interesting but previously unknown (Murakami, Mori, and Orihara, 2008).

Example

Solomon and Bronstein (2016) used a web-based, closed-ended questionnaire, to understand the role of serendipity in legal information seeking. While their motivation for research was grounded in understanding the phenomenon of serendipity, their study design, which includes questions relating to the use of electronic, printed, and human information sources, also informs research relating to physical vs. digital research and strategies for information behaviors in the context of legal information seeking. Participants included 135 Israeli family law advocates, a 22.5% response rate. The survey included Likert scale and multiple choice questions relating, for example, to the frequency in which participants experience unexpected and valuable encounters (based on Bogers and Björneborn, 2013), participants' "background problems" (Erdelez, 2004, 2005), and the value of the encounters. Solomon and Bronstein (2016) found that family law advocates were "super-encounters" (Erdelez, 1999) who perceived electronic information sources (e.g., electronic databases, the web) to be the most serendipitous sources. While Solomon and Bronstein (2016) note questionnaires' dependence on participants to recall their information encountering experiences as a potential drawback, they argue it would be difficult to observe the phenomenon of serendipity; this is particularly true given the time constraints of this study population, family law advocates.

5.7   LOGFILE ANALYSIS

Background

In serendipity research relating to digital environments, computer logs are often combined with other methods including pre- and post-task or post-session questionnaires (e.g., Benjamin et al., 2014), interviews (e.g., Åman et al., 2014), and verbal protocols (e.g., Toms, 1997). A computer log (or transaction log) records all time-stamped actions that users make and all responses from the system, as well as selected metadata.

Use in Serendipity Research

Logfiles are actively used in the digital use environment as they identify user actions (e.g., keystrokes and mouse clicks) and systems responses and thus tend to be used for the following purposes identified in Table 5.1:

> 6. develop and test cues to trigger the phenomena,

> 7. develop and test techniques to facilitate connections and relationships that have the potential to enable the phenomena, and

> 8. develop and test techniques to facilitate a serendipitous interpretation of the connections, i.e., get to the valuable outcome.

Logfile analysis has been used in serendipity research in a number of ways, both inside and outside a lab. André et al. (2009b), for example, collected client-side web search logs over a period of one month from 36 participants together with interviews and questionnaires. The logs led the researchers to compare participants' explicit serendipity judgments (defined as interesting but not relevant results) with actual interactions with their desktop including interactions with desktop content. They found that "rather than harming serendipity, personalization appears to identify interesting results in addition to relevant ones" (p. 2033). In contrast, Taramigkou, Apostolou, and Mentza's (2017), the research took place within a lab setting. We examine this latter research in more detail to understand the value of the method they selected.

The motivations behind Taramigkou et al.'s (2017) research were two of the six main motivations of serendipity research identified in Chapter 2: information overload and user experience. They argue:

> *Despite the vast amount of potentially inspiring information available on the Web and the social Web and the emergence of specialized inspiration engines, it is not easy for users to discover inspirational information among the results list of engines that follow the conventional search paradigm in which users type in their queries and*

the engine presents a list of results leaving it to the user to go through each result and possibly discover an inspiration resource by reading the results previews (p. 94).

While there is a lot of information available on the web and through social media platforms, discovering that information is generally accomplished following the direct search paradigm; alternative search paradigms are needed to support serendipity.

Example

Taramigkou et al. (2017) conducted two task-based experiments in a lab and a pilot study to evaluate how well their experimental system, CReative User centric Inspirational SEarch (CRUISE), supported "serendipitous encounters" (p. 107). Only the first study in which log data was analyzed is explored here.

In the first task-based user study reported by Taramigkou et al. (2017), using a between-subjects design, participants used an experimental system, CRUISE, or the baseline system. Interactions with these systems were logged for analysis. The baseline system was a standard query-based retrieval system through which users could type queries and view results (documents, images, videos) in a list. In contrast, CRUISE was designed to support serendipity, recommending diverse sources through visual cues and allowing users to interactively explore information drawn from the web as well as a microblogging site (Twitter). Twenty Ph.D. students were asked to complete a task to create an outline for a research proposal and complete a post-study questionnaire designed to assess the systems based on, for example, the quality of the content. Participants were randomly assigned to either the focus or control group and asked to evaluate their respective systems on their support for inspiration and serendipity (usefulness and unexpectedness of results). Two professors assessed the originality and quality of the theses outlines. Taramigkou et al. (2017) hypothesized that those participants "who had serendipitous discoveries would be inspired and hence able to formulate creative ideas" (p. 107). The data logged during the user studies allowed Taramigkou et al. (2017) to compare participant interactions with the experimental and baseline system and find that participants performed significantly more queries when using the experimental system and that the experimental system was more serendipitous than the baseline system, measured using the log data collected and a metric for assessing serendipity in recommendation systems adapted from Ge et al. (2010).

The two professors' assessments also suggested use of the experimental system led to better outcomes both in terms of quality and originality. Like Martin and Quan-Haase (2016), Taramigkou et al. (2017) noted that participant recruitment was a challenge and the limited number of participants led to changes in their methodology. Taramigkou et al. (2017) also noted privacy concerns that some participants expressed in the use of individual Twitter accounts, through which the recommendation service was based. But, overall, it appears, that observation through log analysis, together with other methods, provided a detailed record of user interactions. Log analysis provided an unobtrusive method of observing interactions rather than solely relying on participants' memory of these interactions, helping to confirm findings from professor assessments and the questionnaire.

5.8 MEASURING SERENDIPITY?

We are confident in saying that we cannot yet measure serendipity and we are still a long way from being able to predict its occurrence. Serendipity can be a lengthy process from that first observation of a cue that sets off a trigger, to that valuable outcome. Thus, any notion of outcomes and their success may be a long time in the making, which is often not very conducive to research, and constrains application developments in the digital information environment.

To examine the measurement issue in the digital information environment, we focus on the set of elements from Chapter 4 that can be quantified. Our approach to this matter follows a positivist paradigm, and does ignore the initial purposes that relate to understanding the phenomena, which is populated primarily by qualitative research. It is not intended to assess, for example, the context or the individual differences of users, which have been well documented within their respective disciplines and for which serendipity is just another problem area. Instead, we have focused on measuring items essential to, and clearly defined within, a study of serendipity. This includes a look at assessing the environment as a whole, the cue that drives the trigger and subsequently the connections, which hopefully will lead to that valuable outcome.

- **Holistic assessment of the digital information environment**, that is, does it have the potential capability of facilitating serendipity?

  McCay-Peet and colleagues (McCay-Peet, Toms and Kelloway, 2014; McCay-Peet and Toms, 2015; McCay-Peet, Toms and Kelloway, 2015) identified the characteristics of digital information environments conducive to serendipity and created a 15-item scale, the *Serendipitous Digital Environment Scale* (see Appendix A) that includes four dimensions or factors (Leads to the Unexpected, Highlights Triggers, Trigger-Rich, and Enables Connections). The four dimensions primarily capture the trigger/connection stage and unexpected element identified across multiple models of serendipity in Table 3.1. When used in conjunction with a 4-item *Perception of Serendipity Scale* (McCay-Peet, Toms and Kelloway, 2015), an assessment of how frequently a user perceives serendipity occurs in a digital information environment may be obtained, thus capturing serendipity in a more holistic manner. The *Perception of Serendipity Scale* (see Appendix B) includes items that are essentially definitions of serendipity; two items use the word "serendipity" while two describe the phenomenon, mirroring definitions developed by Erdelez (2005) and Makri and Blandford (2012). Both the *Serendipitous Digital Environment* and *Perception of Serendipity* scales are measured on a 5-point scale of agreement (strongly agree, disagree, neither agree nor disagree, agree, strongly agree). However, more work still needs to be done to validate the scales.

- **Enable the "anomaly"** or the chance encounter to trigger an event.

  Enabling a chance encounter has two characteristics:

  ○ the ability of the cue to attract the user's attention, and

  ○ the ability of the cue to engage the user with its content.

  To date, this has been measured by a number of measures such as Unexpectedness (Adamopolos and Tuzhilin, 2014), Originality (Koh et al., 2007), Interestingness (André et al., 2009a), and Novelty (Toms, 2000b). Not all measures are fully described in their papers making it difficult to extract operational measures. Some are objective measures, and some assess user perception. Toms (2000b), for example, measured Novelty as the percentage of articles read on topics previously unknown to participants, while Interestingness was rated using a user perception scale.

  The *Serendipitous Digital Environment Scale* (discussed above) has three dimensions that deal specifically with the triggers and their value: Trigger-Rich, Highlights Triggers, and Leads to the Unexpected (McCay-Peet, Toms, and Kelloway, 2015).

- **Support the user in "connecting the dots,"** that is, identifying the relationship between the cue and what is percolating inside the user's head, or showing relationships between the cue and other incongruent elements.

  Enabling this function requires the development of a tool to assess the user in recognizing that relationship. We can evaluate the tool's ability to identify connections as well as the user's perception of the usefulness of the tool's output. The *Serendipitous Digital Environment Scale* discussed above has one dimension that deals specifically with the user's perception of whether the environment enables connections, but this examines the environment holistically and not the output of a single tool.

- **Support the user in reaching a significant surprise outcome.**

  Similarly, this too requires tools that aid the user in making sense of the connection. To our knowledge no tool yet achieves this, and thus we have no measures, but we surmise that this will be somewhat similar to the previous one.

- **The valuable outcome.**

  In most qualitative research, the presence or lack of, a valuable outcome is often a question asked of participants. Indeed, a positive response is a measurable indicator that serendipity has occurred (pending the presence of the other conditions, as simply being a surprise is not sufficient). A successful valuable and unexpected outcome may be the ultimate measure.

Because the bulk of the research on serendipity to date has focused on understanding the phenomena, we do not have specific measures that have been operationalized and tested for reliability and validity. But that research provides some hints. Makri and Blandford (2012), for example, identified *insightful* and *valuable*, but did not prescribe how each could be measured.

5.9   SUMMARY

Evident from a review of the methods used in serendipity research is that each technique has the ability, to varying degrees, to inform our understanding of the phenomenon, what may facilitate it, and help evaluate how well an environment facilitates it. While some of the methods discussed in this chapter seem better able to help us gain an understanding of serendipity such as interviews, other methods such as analysis of log data appear to be more useful for the evaluation of systems designed to support serendipity. However, what is evident from the research examined in this chapter is that there is flexibility in the use of methods and a great deal of room for creativity in the development of approaches to serendipity research. A lessened reliance on memory is particularly important in serendipity research as participants may have difficulty recalling the details surrounding their information encounters (Erdelez and Rioux, 2000b). Using a mixed methods approach appears to be the most fruitful tactic to take in the study of serendipity, no matter the motivation for the research or its context. Serendipity is difficult to facilitate and capture, however, "if you want to understand serendipity there is value in coming at serendipity from many different directions" (André et al., 2009a, p. 307).

CHAPTER 6

Conclusion and Framework

This book has examined serendipity through a digital information environment lens. It comes at a critical juncture in the development of this relatively nascent research area. Although research papers on serendipity in digital information environments have been bubbling up in conference proceedings and journals across a variety of disciplines for decades now, they are on the increase and patterns are developing in the way the research is approached. We identified several of these patterns including the drivers of serendipity research and how serendipity is approached in the research, facilitated, and measured. These patterns provide frameworks for future research and reveal scarcity in some areas pointing to areas in which more work is needed.

Drivers. The rationale for conducting serendipity research is expanding as society reckons with technological developments in digital information environments and their implications. We are still grappling with the shift from physical to digital, although this may change in the coming decades. Information overload and filter bubbles are problems that are likely to continue to dog users in the coming years and more research will be needed to ensure good user experience and develop user strategies for increasing the potential for serendipity. Moreover, more research is needed to understand the phenomenon itself, with all its moving parts and its shifting conceptual meaning as a part of living language. More work is also needed to understand the consequences, both good and bad, of trying to turn up the volume on serendipity. What are the privacy and ethical implications, for example, of this form of manipulation through personalization, however good its intentions?

Approaches to serendipity. It is clear there are numerous ways in which serendipity has been approached in research, as both a quality (an event, something, someone) and a process. These different approaches can largely be explained from a research area or discipline perspective. For example, it is no surprise that recommender systems research approaches serendipity as a quality of the something (i.e., the recommendation). While much has been learned through this focus on a specific aspect of support for serendipity, working in interdisciplinary teams with researchers from psychology, information science, and human-computer interaction, for example, may suggest new ways of approaching serendipity, thus building theory.

Facilitating serendipity. Once one moves from the physical setting to one that is an almost exclusively digital information environment, the way in which serendipity can be nurtured and facilitated opens up almost untold (and not yet developed) options. Notably, the digital environment (at present) constrains the process (e.g., viewing options through a multitude of devices with varied sizes of "windows"—the tip of the iceberg phenomena) and at the same time, greatly enhances and augments human capability (along the lines of Licklider's (1960) and Bush's (1945) early predictions) for increased serendipitous encounters and outcomes—as long as the technology does not continue down the filter bubble pathway. With computing capability that has changed since even the writing of this paragraph, we have so much potential for facilitating not just a functional approach to information tasks and knowledge work, but to creating effective nurturing environments that let serendipity happen. Achieving an integrated interface that enables task functionality and at the same time enables serendipity is the "holy grail" of serendipity R&D goals. While we work toward that functionality, the key building blocks are currently in their R&D naissance. Many things have been tested, but we do not yet have a definitive set. We still need tools that:

1. enable anomalies and incongruities;

2. identify the relationships—the connections and bisociations—among different concepts;

3. identify potential outcomes given a set of connections and bisociations; and

4. integrate the three with the user application.

Please note that we are not advocating systems that simply do the task; instead we promote the role of taking advantage of human vagaries, knowledge and experiences that may still inspire solutions that machines do not know about, and that inform and support quality of life.

Methods and measurement. So many methods have been used to understand serendipity as phenomena, mostly the traditional ones that have stood the test of time in many disciplines. In the digital information environments and in particular with respect to serendipity, we are constrained by the human participant and that participant's life history. While the interconnected Web weaves a rich "back channel" of data and information about a person, it still does not know the human experience from one human interaction with a technology to another, and nor does it know the thoughts and perceptions that percolate at the same time. While technology evolves to facilitate human interactions in digital information environments, the tools we use for data collection also continue to advance. However, we need more sophisticated biometric data collection tools that can measure and predict human response, and identify the human response to stimuli. We are almost at the point of being able to monitor and analyze human interactions in a large scale (as the big data phenomenon has presented), which may enable longitudinal collection of human responses, such that we can identify when a human responds to a trigger, and when that valuable outcome has been achieved.

Conceptualization and operationalization. The cornerstone of good research is an ability to precisely describe the phenomenon that will be "placed under the microscope," and then to be able to describe, measure, predict and explain something about that phenomenon. The naysayers may complain about the need for fuzziness in dealing with intangible concepts; they are indeed correct, at least for now. Until we understand fully understand the phenomenon (as well as clearly conceptually and operationally define it, which we have done in this volume) there will be fuzziness. When we introduce policies into organizations, or invest in new applications, or recommend to people about the value of using an application or adopting a type of behavior to advocate and invest in serendipity, then we need to be precise, as there is much at stake. We have a lot of research outcomes in which the serendipitous claim is being made. This is especially so and well articulated in science and engineering. In the social sciences, we have diluted the concept (and particular in the digital information environment) such that anything that is a surprise or unexpected is perceived to be serendipitous. But is that unexpected item in a results list, for example, serendipitous? We need to fully define the scope if we are to do comparative research and meta analyzes that develop a solid foundation on which to build.

Appendix A

The Serendipitous Digital Environment Scale

Purpose: In addition to evaluating the environment, the scales are also useful for comparing digital information environments and for testing relationships with other variables such as personality traits.

Factors and items of the *Serendipitous Digital Environment* scale (McCay-Peet, Toms, and Kelloway, 2015). Measured on a 5-point scale of agreement (strongly agree, disagree, neither agree nor disagree, agree, strongly agree).

Leads to the Unexpected: A user's assessment of the degree to which a digital environment provides opportunities for unexpected interactions with information, ideas, or resources

1. I bump into unexpected content in [the digital information environment].

2. I come across content by chance in [the digital information environment].

3. I am exposed to unanticipated content in [the digital information environment].

4. I stumble upon information in [the digital information environment].

5. I encounter the unexpected in [the digital information environment].

Trigger-Rich: A user's assessment of the degree to which a digital environment contains a variety of information, ideas, or resources that is interesting and useful to the user.

6. [The digital information environment] is full of information useful to me.

7. I find information of value to me in [the digital information environment].

8. [The digital information environment] is a treasure trove of information.

Highlights Triggers: A user's assessment of the degree to which a digital environment brings interesting and useful information, ideas, or resources to the user's attention.

9. [The digital information environment] has features that draw my attention to information.

10. [The digital information environment] has features that alert me to information.

11. [The digital information environment] has features that ensure that my attention is drawn to useful information.

12. I am pointed toward content in [the digital information environment].

Enables Connections: A user's assessment of the degree to which a digital environment makes relationships or connections between information, ideas, or resources apparent.

13. I can see connections between topics in [the digital information environment].

14. [The digital information environment] enables me to make connections between ideas.

15. I come to understand relationships between ideas in [the digital information environment].

Appendix B

Items of the *Perception of Serendipity Scale* (McCay-Peet, Toms, and Kelloway, 2015). Measured on a 5-point scale of agreement (strongly agree, disagree, neither agree nor disagree, agree, strongly agree).

1. In [digital information environment], I experience serendipity that has an impact on my everyday life.

2. In [digital information environment], I experience serendipity that has an impact on my work.

3. I encounter useful information, ideas, or resources that I am not looking for when I use [digital information environment].*

4. In [digital information environment], I experience mixes of unexpectedness and insight that lead to valuable, unanticipated outcomes.**

Note:
*Item adapted from Erdelez's (2005) definition of information encountering;
**Item adapted from Makri and Blandford's (2012) elements of serendipity.

Bibliography

Adamopoulos, P. and Tuzhiln, A. (2014). On unexpectedness in recommender systems: or how to better expect the unexpected. *ACM Transactions on Intelligent Systems and Technology* 5(4), Article 54. DOI: 10.1145/2559952. 41, 61

Ahn, J. and Pierce, J.S. (2005). SEREFE: Serendipitous file exchange between users and devices. In *Proceedings of the 7th International Conference on Human Computer Interaction with Mobile Devices and Services (MobileHCI'05)*, Salzburg, Austria (pp. 39–46). New York: ACM Press. DOI: 10.1145/1085777.1085785. 18, 31

Åman, P., Liikkanen, L.A., Jacucci, G., and Hinkka, A. (2014). OUTMedia: Symbiotic service for music discovery in urban augmented reality. In G. Jacucci et al. (Eds.), *Symbiotic 2014, LNCS 8820*, pp. 61–71. Cham, Switzerland: Springer International Publishing. DOI: 10.1007/978-3-319-13500-7_5. 14, 26, 27, 29, 58

André, P., Schraefel, M. C., Teevan, J., and Dumais, S. T. (2009a). Discovery is never by chance: Designing for (un)serendipity. *Creativity & Cognition* '09, 305–314. DOI: 10.1145/1640233.1640279. 17, 40, 61, 62

André, P., Teevan, J., and Dumais, S. T. (2009b). From x-rays to silly putty via Uranus: Serendipity and its role in web search. *Proceedings of the 27th International Conference on Human Factors in Computing Systems*, 2033–2036. DOI: 10.1145/1518701.1519009. 16, 17, 18, 26, 27, 29, 49, 57, 58

Arvo, J. (1999). Computer aided serendipity: the role of autonomous assistants in problem solving. In *Proceedings of Graphics Interface '99*, Kingsotn, Ontrio, Jun, pp. 183–192. DOI: 10.20380/GI1999.24. 4

Barber, B. and Fox, R. C. (1958). The case of the floppy-eared rabbits: An instance of serendipity gained and serendipity lost. The *American Journal of Sociology* 64(2), 128–136. DOI: 10.1086/222420. 5, 30, 49

Barta, T. (2014). The high cost of not finding information: Rebooted [blog post]. Retrieved from http://www.semantacorp.com/news/2015/1/20/the-high-cost-of-not-finding-information-reboote. 14

Bashyam, H. (2007). Lewis Thomas and droopy rabbit ears. *Journal of Experimental Medicine* 204(12), 2777. DOI: 10.1084/jem.20412fta. 6

Bawden, D. (1986). Information systems and the stimulation of creativity. *Journal of Information Science* 12, 203–216. DOI: 10.1177/016555158601200501. 43

Behavior. (n.d.). In Merriam-Webster online. Retrieved August 29, 2016, from http://www.merriam-webster.com/dictionary/behavior. 30

Bell, E. (2016). The truth about Brexit didn't stand a chance in the online bubble. *The Guardian*. Retrieved from https://www.theguardian.com/media/2016/jul/03/facebook-bubble-brexit-filter. 16

Bellotti, V., Begole, B., Chi, E.H., Ducheneaut, N., Fang, J, Isaacs, E., King, T., Newman, M.W., Partridge, K., Price, B., Rasmussen, P., Roberts, M., Schiano, D.J., and Walendowski, A. (2008). Activity-based serendipitous recommendations with the Magitti mobile leisure guide. In *Proceedings of the SIGCHI Conference on Human Factors in Computing Systems (CHI '08)*. ACM, New York, pp. 1157–1166. DOI: 10.1145/1357054.1357237. 15, 19, 49, 50

Benjamin, W., Chandrasegaran, S., Ramanujan, D., Elmqvist, N., Vishwanathan, S.V.N, and Ramani, K. (2014). Juxtapoze: Supporting serendipity and creative expression in clipart compositions. In *Proceedings of the SIGCHI Conference on Human Factors in Computing Systems (CHI '14)*. ACM, New York, pp. 341–350. DOI: 10.1145/2556288.2557327. 15, 16, 17, 27, 44, 58

Bentley, F.R., Basapur, S. and Chowdhury, S.K. (2011). Promoting intergenerational communication through location-based asynchronous video communication. In *Proceedings of the 13th international conference on Ubiquitous computing (UbiComp '11)*. ACM, New York, pp. 31–40. DOI: 10.1145/2030112.2030117. 19, 51

Bernier, C.L. (1960). Correlative indexes VI: Serendipity, suggestiveness, and display. *American Documentation* 11(4), 277–287. DOI: 10.1002/asi.5090110402. 47

Bilandzic, M., Schroeter, R., and Foth, M. (2013). Gelatine: Making coworking places gel for better collaboration and social learning. In *Proceedings of the 25th Australian Computer-Human Interaction Conference: Augmentation, Application, Innovation, Collaboration (OzCHI '13)*, Haifeng Shen, Ross Smith, Jeni Paay, Paul Calder, and Theodor Wyeld (Eds.). ACM, New York, NY, USA, 427-436. DOI: 10.1145/2541016.2541027. 31

Björneborn, L. (2008). Serendipity dimensions and users' information behavior in the physical library interface. *Information Research* 13(4). Retrieved from http://informationr.net/ir/13-4/paper370.html. 48, 49, 55

Björneborn, L. (2010). Design dimensions enabling divergent behavior across physical, digital, and social library interfaces, in T. Ploug, P. Hasle, and Oinas-Kukkonen (eds) *Persuasive*

2010, Lecture Notes in Computer Science 6137, pp. 143–149. DOI: 10.1007/978-3-642-13226-1_15. 40

Boden, M.A. (1990a). *The Creative Mind: Myths and Mechanisms*. London: Weidenfield and Nicholson. 43

Boden, M.A. (1990b). *Dimensions of Creativity*. MIT Press.

Boden, M.A. (1996). Agents and creativity. In B. Gorayska and J.L. Mey (eds.), *Cognitive Technology: In search of a Humane Intrface*, pp. 119–127. Elsevier Science. DOI: 10.1016/S0166-4115(96)80027-6. 6, 41

Bogdan, R. (1973). Participant observation. *Peabody Journal of Education* 50(4), 302–308. DOI: 10.1080/01619567309537925.

Bogers, T. and Björneborn, L. (2013). Micro-serendipity: Meaningful coincidences in everyday life shared on Twitter. In *Proc. iConference 2013*, pp. 196–208. DOI: 10.9776/13175. 21, 57

Bordino, I., Lalmas, M., Mejova, Y., and Van Laere, O. (2014). Driving curiosity in search with large-scale entity networks. *SIGWEB Newsletter*, Autumn, Article 5, pp. 1–12. DOI: 10.1145/2682914.2682919. 19, 26, 27, 29

Bordino, I., Mejova, Y, and Lalmas, M. (2013a). Penguins in sweaters, or serendipitous entity search on user-generated content. In *Proceedings of the 22nd ACM international conference on Information and Knowledge Management (CIKM '13). ACM*, New York, pp. 19–118. DOI: 10.1145/2505515.2505680. 29, 31

Bordino, I., Morales, G. de F., Weber, I. and Bonchi, F. (2013b). From machu_picchu to "rafting the urubamba river": Anticipating information needs via the entity-query graph. In *Proceedings of the sixth ACM international conference on Web search and data mining (WSDM '13)*. ACM, New York, pp. 275-284. DOI: 10.1145/2433396.2433433. 29, 31

Brown, C., Efstratiou, C., Leontiadis, I., Quercia, D., and Mascolo, C. (2014). Tracking serendipitous interactions: How individual cultures shape the office. In *Proceedings of the 17th ACM Conference on Computer Supported Cooperative Work and Social Computing (CSCW '14)*. ACM, New York, pp. 1072–1081. DOI: 10.1145/2531602.2531641. 13

Bush, V. (1945). As we may think. *The Atlantic Monthly*. (https://www.theatlantic.com/magazine/archive/1945/07/as-we-may-think/303881/). 63

Campanario, J. (1996). Using Citation Classics to study the incidence of serendipity in scientific discovery. *Scientometrics* 37(1), 3–24. DOI: 10.1007/bf02093482. 53

Campos, J. A. and Figueiredo, A. D. (2002). Programming for serendipity. Paper presented at the *Proceedings of the 2002 AAAI Fall Symposium*. DOI: 10.2139/ssrn.1385402. 6, 33, 42, 57

Cannon, W.B. (1945). *The Way of an Investigator*. New York: Norton. 3

Chandra, S. and Yu, X. (2011). An empirical analysis of serendipitous media sharing among campus-wise wireless users. *ACM Transactions on Multimedia Computing Communications and Applications* 7(1), Article 6. DOI: 10.1145/1870121.1870127.

Chen, H., Yim, T., and Fye, D. (1995). Automatic thesaurus generation for an electronic community system. *Journal of the American Society for Information Science* 46(3), 175–193. DOI: 10.1002/(SICI)1097-4571(199504)46:3<175::AID-ASI3>3.0.CO;2-U.

Cleverley, P.H. and Burnett, S. (2015a). Creating sparks: Comparing search results using discriminatory search term word co-occurrence to facilitate serendipity in the enterprise. *Journal of Information and Knowledge Management* 14(1), 1–27. DOI: 10.1142/S0219649215500070. 15, 22, 27

Cleverley, P.H. and Burnett, S. (2015b). Retrieving haystacks: A data driven information needs model for faceted search. *Journal of Information Science* 41(1), 97–113. DOI: 10.1177/0165551514554522.

Cooper, J., Lewis, R., and Urquhart, C. (2004). Using participant or non-participant observation to explain information behavior. *Information Research* 9(4). Retrieved from http://informationr.net/ir/9-4/paper184.html.

Corneli, J., Pease, A., Colton, S. Jordanous, A., Guckelsberger, C. (2016). Modelling serendipity in a computational context. Retrieved from arXiv:1411.0440v4 [cs.AI]. 23, 24, 25, 28

Cunha, M.P.E. (2005). Serendipity: Why some organizations are luckier than others. *FEUNL Working Paper* no. 472. DOI: 10.2139/ssrn.882782. 33, 36

Cunha, M.P.e., Rego, A., Clegg, S. and Lindsay, G. (2014). The dialectics of serendipity. *European Management Journal* 33: 9–18. DOI: 10.1016/j.emj.2014.11.001. 8

Danzico, L. (2010). The design of serendipity is not by chance. *Interactions* 17(5), 16–18. 4

de Bono, E. (1970). *Lateral Thinking: Creativity Step-by Step*. Penguin. 42

De Bruijn, O. and Spence, R. (2008). A new framework for theory-based interaction design applied to serendipitous information retrieval. *ACM Transactions on Computer-Human Interaction* 15(5), Article 5. DOI: 10.1145/1352782.1352787. 16, 27, 31

De Bruijn, O. and Spence, R. (2001). Serendipity within a ubiquitous computing environment: a case for opportunistic browsing. In G.D. Abowd and B. Brumitt, and S.A.N. Shafer (Eds). *Ubicomp 2001. Lecture Note in Computer Science 2201*, pp. 362–369. 41

de Figueiredo, A.D. and Campos, J. (2001). The serendipity equations, In *Proceedings of the Workshop program at the Fourth International Conference on Case-Based Reasoning, ICCBR 2001*.

Washington, DC: naval Research Laboratory, Navy Center for Applied Research in Artificial Intelligence, pp. 121–124. 8

De Rond, M. (2014). The structure of serendipity. *Culture and Organization* 20(5), 342–358. DOI: 10.1080/14759551.2014.967451. 1, 8

Dervin, B. and Foreman-Wernet, L. (2003). *Sense-making Methodology Reader: Selected Writings of Brenda Dervin*. Cresskill, NJ: Hampton Press. 21

Eagle, N. and Pentland, A. (2005). Social serendipity: mobilizing social software. *Pervasive Computing*, 28–34. DOI: 10.1109/MPRV.2005.37. 44

Ellis, D. (2005). Ellis's model of information seeking behavior. In K.E. Fisher, S. Erdelez, and L. McKechnie (Eds.), *Theories of Information Behavior* (pp. 138–142). Medford, NJ: Information Today.

Eppler, M. and Mengis, J. (2004). The concept of information overload: A review of literature from Organization Science, Accounting, Marketing, MIS, and related disciplines. Information Society, 20(5), 325–344. DOI: 10.1080/01972240490507974. 14, 15

Erdelez, S. (1996). Information encountering on the Internet. In M. E. Williams (Ed.), *Proceedings of the 17th National Online Meeting* (pp. 101–108). Medford, NJ: Learned Information, Inc. 14, 20, 30, 31

Erdelez, S. (1997). Information encountering: A conceptual framework for accidental information discovery. In P. Vakkari, R. Savolainen, S. Erdelez, and B. Dervin (Eds.), *Information Seeking in Context* (pp. 412–421). London: Taylor Graham. 21, 30

Erdelez, S. (1999). Information enountering: It's more than just bumping into information. *American Society for Information Science* 25(3), 25–29. 30, 31, 57

Erdelez, S. (2000). Towards understanding information encountering on the Web. *Proceedings of the ASIS Annual Meeting* 37, 363–371. 36

Erdelez, S. (2004). Investigation of information encountering in the controlled research environment. *Information Processing and Management* 40(6), 1013–1025. DOI: 10.1016/j.ipm.2004.02.002. 26, 31, 47, 57

Erdelez, S. (2005). Information encountering. In K.E. Fisher, S. Erdelez, and L. McKechnie (Eds.), *Theories of Information Behavior* (pp. 179–185). Medford, NJ: Information Today. 21, 57, 60, 69

Erdelez, S. and Rioux, K. (2000a). Sharing tools on newspaper web sites: An exploratory study. *Online Information Review* 24(3), 218–228. DOI: 10.1108/14684520010341290. 24, 30

Erdelez, S. and Rioux, K. (2000b). Sharing information encountered for others on the web. *The New Review of Information Behavior Research* 1, 219–223. 24, 30, 62

Erdelez, S., Heinström, J., Makri, S., Björneborn, L., Beheshti, J., Toms, E., and Agarwal, N. K. (2016). Research perspectives on serendipity and information encountering. *Proceedings of the Association for Information Science and Technology (ASIS&T)* 53, 1–5. DOI: 10.1002/pra2.2016.14505301011. 53

Event. (n.d.). In *Merriam-Webster* online. Retrieved August 29, 2016, from http://www.merriam-webster.com/dictionary/event. 26

Fan, X., Mostafa, J., Mane, K. and Sugimoto, C. (2012). Personalization is not a panacea: Balancing serendipity and personalization in medical news content delivery. In *Proceedings of the 2nd ACM SIGHIT International Health Informatics Symposium (IHI '12)*. ACM, New York, pp. 709–714. DOI: 10.1145/2110363.2110445. 16

Fine, G.A. and Deegan, J.G. (1996). Three principles of Serendip: insight, chance, and discovery in qualitative research. *International Journal of Qualitative Studies in Education* 9(4), 443–447. DOI: 10.1080/0951839960090405. 1, 5

Fish, R.S., Kraut, R.E., Root, R.W., and Rice, R.E. (1993). Video as a technology for informal communication. *Communications of the ACM* 36(1), pp. 48–61. DOI: 10.1145/151233.151237.

Fleming, A. (1964). Penicillin. *Nobel Lecture*, December 11, 1945 (https://www.nobelprize.org/nobel_prizes/medicine/laureates/1945/fleming-lecture.pdf). 5

Flory, P. (1977). Paul Flory on basic research. *Chemical and Engineering News* 55(9), 4. DOI: 10.1021/cen-v055n009.p004. 4

Ford, N. (1999). Information retrieval and creativity: Towards support for the original thinker. *Journal of Documentation* 55(5), 528–542. DOI: 10.1108/EUM0000000007156. 41, 43

Forsblom, A., Nurmi, P., Åman, P. and Liikkanen, L. (2012). Out of the bubble: Serendipitous even recommendations at an urban music festival. In *Proceedings of the 2012 ACM International Conference on Intelligent User Interfaces (IUI '12)*. ACM, New York, pp. 253–256. DOI: 10.1145/2166966.2167011. 17

Foster, A. and Ford, N. (2003). Serendipity and information seeking: An empirical study. *Journal of Documentation* 59(3), 321–340. DOI: 10.1108/00220410310472518. 4, 8, 42, 47

Frohlich, D.M., Wall, S., and Kiddle, G. (2013). Rediscovery of forgotten images in domestic photo collections. *Personal and Ubiquitous Computing* 17(4), 729–740. DOI: 10.1007/s00779-012-0612-4. 13, 27, 30, 31

Ge, M., Delgado-Battenfeld, C., and Jannach, D. (2010). Beyond accuracy: Evaluating recommender systems by coverage and serendipity. In *Proceedings of the Fourth ACM Conference on Recommender Systems,* Barcelona, Spain (pp. 257–260), ACM. DOI: 10.1145/1864708.1864761. 59

Glaser, B. and Strauss, A. (1967). *The Discovery of Grounded Theory: Strategies for Qualitative Inquiry.* Chicago: Aldine. 50

Gordon, M.D. and Dumais, S. (1998). Using laentic emantic indexing for literature based discovery. *Journal of the American Society for Information Science and Technology* 49(8), 674–685. DOI: 10.1002/(SICI)1097-4571(199806)49:8<674::AID-ASI2>3.0.CO;2-T. 42

Guy, I., Levin, R., Daniel, T., and Bolshinsky, E. (2015). Islands in the stream: A study of item recommendation within an enterprise social stream. In *Proceedings of the 38th International ACM SIGIR Conference on Research and Development in Information Retrieval (SIGIR '15).* ACM, New York, pp. 665–674. DOI: 10.1145/2766462.2767746. 13, 15, 17, 29, 57

Gyllstrom, K. and Moens, M.-F. (2012). Surfin' Wikipedia: An analysis of the Wikipedia (non-random) surfer's behavior from aggregate. In *Proceedings of the 4th Information Interaction in Context Symposium (IIIX '12).* New York, ACM, pp. 155–163. DOI: 10.1145/2362724.2362752. 31

Halacy, D. (1967). *Science and Serendipity: Great Discoveries by Accident.* Philadepphia: Macrae Smith Company. 8

Hangal, S., Nagpal, A., and Lam, M. (2012). Effective browsing and serendipitous discovery with an experience-infused browser. In *Proceedings of the 2012 ACM International Conference on Intelligent User Interfaces (IUI '12).* New York, ACM, pp. 149–158. DOI: 10.1145/2166966.2166994. 22

Hank, C., Jordan, M. W., and Wildemuth, B. M. (2009). Survey research. In B. M. Wildemuth (Ed.), *Applications of Social Research Methods to Questions in Information and Library Science* (pp. 256–269). Westport, CT : Libraries Unlimited. DOI: 10.1016/j.jss.2008.11.747. 56

Heinström, J. (2006). Psychological factors behind incidental information acquisition. *Library and Information Science Research* 28(4), 579–594. DOI: 10.1016/j.lisr.2006.03.022. 18, 20, 29, 31, 47, 57

Herrmann, N. (1989). *The Creative Brain.* Brain Books. DOI: 10.1002/j.2162-6057.1991.tb01140.x. 6

Hornung, T., Ziegler, C.-N., Franz, S., Przyjaciel-Zablocki, M., Schätzle, A., and Lausen, G. (2013). Evaluating hybrid music recommender systems. In *Proceedings of the 2013 IEEE/*

WIC/ACM International Joint Conferences on Web Intelligence (WI) and Intelligent Agent Technologies (IAT) (WI-IAT '13) (pp. 57–64). IEEE Computer Society, Washington, DC. DOI: 10.1109/WI-IAT.2013.9. 15, 29, 57

Hristova, D., Williams, M.J., Musolesi, M., Panzarasa, P. and Mascolo, C. (2016). Measuring urban social diversity using interconnected geo-social networks. In *Proceedings of the 25th International Conference on World Wide Web (WWW '16)*. International World Wide Web Conferences Steering Committee, Republic and Canton of Geneva, Switzerland, pp. 21–30. DOI: 10.1145/2872427.2883065. 19, 29

Huldtgren, A., Mayer, C., Kierepka, O., and Geiger, C. (2014). Towards serendipitous urban encounters with SoundtrackOfYourLife. In *Proceedings of the 11th Conference on Advances in Computer Entertainment Technology (ACE '14)*. ACM, New York, Article 28. DOI: 10.1145/2663806.2663836. 17, 27

Inkpen, K., Whittaker, S., Czerwinski, M., Fernandez, R., and Wallace, J. (2008). GroupBanter: Supporting serendipitous group conversations with IM. In Bertino, E. and Joshi, J.B.D. (Eds.) *CollaborateCom 2008, Lecture Notes of the Institute from Computer Sciences, Social Informatics and Telecommunications Engineering* (Vol. 10) (pp. 485–498). Spinger. 26, 27

International Data Corporation (2001). The high cost of not finding information. Retrieved from http://www.ejitime.com/materials/IDC%20on%20The%20High%20Cost%20Of%20Not%20Finding%20Information.pdf. 14

International Organization for Standardization [ISO] (2010). *Ergonomics of Human-centered System Interaction: Part 201: Human-centered Design for Interactive Systems* [Reference number ISO 9241–210:2010(E)]. Switzerland: ISO. 18

Jang, H., Choe, S.P., and Song, J. (2011). Exploring serendipitous social networks: Jharing immediate situations among unacquainted individuals. In *Proceedings of the 13th International Conference on Human Computer Interaction with Mobile Devices and Services (MobileHCI '11)* (pp. 513–516). ACM, New York. DOI: 10.1145/2037373.2037449. 28, 29

Jansen, B. J. (2006). Search log analysis: What it is, what's been done, how to do it. *Library and Information Science Research* 28(3), 407–432. DOI: 10.1016/j.lisr.2006.06.005.

Jarvenpaa, S.L. and Lang, K.R. (2005). Managing the paradoxes of mobile technology. *Information Systems Management* 22(4), 7–23. DOI: 10.1201/1078.10580530/45520.22.4.20050901/90026.2. 16

Jeffrey, P. (2000). Forum contact space: serendipity in the workplace. In *CHI '00 Extended Abstracts on Human Factors in Computing Systems (CHI EA '00)*. ACM, New York, NY, USA, pp. 331–332. DOI: 10.1145/633292.633492. 13, 26, 27

Jeffrey, P. and McGrath, A. (2000). Sharing serendipity in the workplace. In *Proceedings of the third international conference on Collaborative virtual environments (CVE '00)*, Elizabeth Churchill and Martin Reddy (Eds.). ACM, New York, NY, USA, 173-179. DOI: 10.1145/351006.351037. 44

Jiang, T., Lui, F., and Chi, Y. (2015). Online information encountering: Modelling the process and influencing factors. *Journal of Documentation* 71(6), 1135–1157. DOI: 10.1108/JD-07-2014-0100. 27

Jones, S. (2015). The ethical blindness of algorithms. Quartz. Retrieved from https://qz.com/343750/the-ethical-blindness-of-algorithms/. 22

Kirman, B., Linehan, C., and Lawson, S. (2012). Get lost: Facilitating serendipitous exploration in location-sharing services. In *CHI '12 Extended Abstracts on Human Factors in Computing Systems (CHI EA '12)* (pp. 2303–2308). ACM, New York. DOI: 10.1145/2212776.2223793. 16, 17, 29, 30

Kito, N., Oku, K., and Kawagoe, K. (2015). Correlation analysis among the metadata-based similarity, acoustic-based distance, and serendipity of music. In *Proceedings of the 19th International Database Engineering and Applications Symposium (IDEAS '15)* (pp. 198–199). ACM, New York. DOI: 10.1145/2790755.2790786.

Koestler, A. (1964). *The Act of Creation*. Hutchinson. 36, 41

Koh, E, Kerne, A. and Hill, R. (2007). Creativity support: information discovery and exploratory search. In *SIGIR'07*, July 23–27, 2007, Amsterdam, Netherlands. 61

Kop, R. (2012). Information aggregation in networked learning: the human factor and serendipity. In *Proceedings of the 8th International Conference on Networked Learning 2012*, p. 178185. 44

Kotkov, D., Wang, S. and Veijalainen, J. (2016). A survey of serendipity in recommender systems. *Knowledge-Based Systems* 111, 180–192. DOI: 10.1016/j.knosys.2016.08.014. 28, 32, 47

Kraut, R., Egido, C., and Galegher, J. (1988). Patterns of contact and communication in scientific research collaboration. In *Proceedings of the 1988 ACM Conference on Computer-supported Cooperative Work (CSCW '88)*. ACM, New York, pp.1–12. DOI: 10.1145/62266.62267. 13

Laquinta, L., Gemmis, M., Lopsand, P. and Semararo, G. (2008). Introducing serendipity in a content based recommender system. *Eighth International Conference On Hybrid Intelligent Systems*, Barcelona, Spain, pp. 168–174. 41

Laplante, A. and Downie, J.S., (2011). The utilitarian and hedonic outcomes of music information-seeking in everyday life. *Library and Information Science Research* 33, 202–210. DOI: 10.1016/j.lisr.2010.11.002.

Leong, T.W. Harper, R. and Regan, T. (2011). Nudging towards serendipity: a case with personal digital photos. *Conference Proceedings, British Computer Society Human–Computer Interaction.* 40

Leong, T.W., Vetere, F., and Howard, S. (2006). Randomness as a resource for design. In *Proceedings of the 6th Conference on Designing Interactive Systems* (pp. 132–139). ACM, New York. 40

Leong, T.W., Vetere, F. and Howard, S. (2005). The serendipity shuffle. In *Proceedings of OZCHI 2005*, Canberra, Australia, November 22–25. 19

Leong, T.W. and Wright, P. (2013). Revisiting social practices surrounding music. In *Proceedings of the SIGCHI Conference on Human Factors in Computing Systems (CHI '13)*. ACM, New York, pp. 951–960. DOI: 10.1145/2470654.2466122.

Leong, T.W., Wright, P., Vetere, F., and Howard, S. (2010). Understanding experience using dialogical methods: The case of serendipity. In *Proceedings of the 22nd Conference of the Computer-Human Interaction Special Interest Group of Australia on Computer-Human Interaction (OZCHI '10)*. ACM, New York, pp.256–263. DOI: 10.1145/1952222.1952278. 19, 27, 33, 49, 51, 52

Leslie, I. (2012). In search of serendipity. *The Economist* (https://www.1843magazine.com/content/ideas/ian-leslie/search-serendipity?page=full). 7

Liang, R-H. (2012). Designing for unexpected encounters with digital products: case studies of serendipity as felt experience. *International Journal of Design* 6(1), 41–58. 33, 40

Licklider, J.C.R. (1960). Man-computer symbiosis. *Transactions on Human Factors in Electronics HFE-1*, 4–11. DOI: 10.1109/THFE2.1960.4503259. 63

Liikkanen, L.A. and Åman, P. (2016). Shuffling services: Current trends in interacting with digital music. *Interacting with Computers* 28(3), 352–371. DOI: 10.1093/iwc/iwv004. 19, 26, 27, 29

Lindsay, G. (2014). How IBM is using Watson and an innovative workspace to crunch big data for big solutions. Retrieved from https://www.fastcoexist.com/3027437/how-ibm-is-using-watson-and-an-innovative-workspace-to-crunch-big-data-for-big-solutions. 13, 14

Lindsay, R.K. and Gordon, M.D. (1999). Literature-based discovery by lexical statistics. *Journal of the American Society for Information Science and Technology* 50(7), 574–587. DOI: 10.1002/(SICI)1097-4571(1999)50:7<574::AID-ASI3>3.0.CO;2-Q. 42

Lu, Q., Chen, T., Zhang, W., Yang, D., Yu, Y. (2012). Serendipitous personalized ranking for top-N recommendation. In *2012 IEEE/WIC?ACM International conference eon Web Intelligence and Intelligent Agent Technology*. DOI: 10.1109/WI-IAT.2012.135. 41

Luo, L., and Wildemuth, B. M. (2009). Semistructured interviews. In B. M. Wildemuth (Ed.), *Applications of Social Research Methods to Questions in Information and Library Science* (pp. 232–241). Westport, CT: Libraries Unlimited. 49

Luxford, J.M. (2009). A fifteenth-century English chronicle source for Robin Hood. *Journal of Medieval History* 35(7), 70–76. DOI: 10.1016/j.jmedhist.2009.01.002. 4

Makri, Blandford, Woods, Sharples, and Maxwell. (2014). "Making my own luck": Serendipity strategies and how to support them in digital information environments. *Journal of the Association for Information Science and Technology* 65(11), 2179–2194. DOI: /10.1002/asi.23200. 18, 20

Makri, S. Bhuiya, J, Carthy, J., and Owusu-Bonsu, J. (2015). Observing serendipity in digital information environments. In *Proceedings of the 78th ASIS&T Annual Meeting: Information Science with Impact: Research in and for the Community (ASIST '15)* (Article 19). American Society for Information Science; Silver Springs, MD. DOI: 10.1002/pra2.2015.145052010019. 55

Makri, S., and Blandford, A. (2012). Coming across information serendipitously - Part 1: A process model. *Journal of Documentation* 68(5), 684–705. DOI: 10.1108/00220411211256030. 4, 21, 23, 24, 25, 47, 60, 62, 69

Maksai, A., Garcin, F., and Faltings, B. (2015). Predicting online performance of news recommender systems through richer evaluation metrics. In *Proceedings of the 9th ACM Conference on Recommender Systems (RecSys '15)*. ACM, New York, pp. 179–186. DOI: 10.1145/2792838.2800184. 17

Martin, K. and Quan-Haase, A. (2013). Are e-books replacing print books? tradition, serendipity, and opportunity in the adoption and use of e-books for historical research and teaching. *Journal of the Association for Information Science and Technology* 64(5), 1016–1028. DOI: 10.1002/asi.22801. 13

Martin, K. and Quan-Haase, A. (2016). The role of agency in historians' experiences of serendipity in physical and digital information environments. *Journal of Documentation* 72(6), 1008–1026. DOI: 10.1108/JD-11-2015-0144. 13, 30, 49, 50, 59

Martinez, K. (2011). 10 hard to translate English words. *LISTVERSE*, July 13, 2011 (http://listverse.com/2011/07/13/10-hard-to-translate-english-words/). 2

Martinez-Pabon, F., Ospina-Quintero, J.C., Garzon-Marin, V., Chantre-Astaiza, A., Muñoz-Organero, M., and Ramirez-Gonzalez, G. (2014). Enriching public displays ads recommendations using an individual-group cooperation model. In Gehring, S. (Ed.), *Proceedings of The International Symposium on Pervasive Displays (PerDis '14)* (pp. 186–187). ACM, New York. DOI: 10.1145/2611009.2617196.

Matt, C., Benlian, A., Hess, T., and Weiß, C. (2014). Escaping from the filter bubble? The effects of novelty and serendipity on users' evaluations of online recommendations. In *Proceedings of the Thirty Fifth International Conference on Information Systems*, Auckland. Retrieved from http://aisel.aisnet.org/icis2014/proceedings/HumanBehavior/67/. 17, 29

McBirnie, A. (2008). Seeking serendipity: The paradox of control. *ASLIB Proceedings* 60(6), 600–618. DOI: 10.1108/00012530810924294. 18, 30, 47, 49, 50

McBirnie, A. and Urquhart, C. (2011). Motifs: dominant interaction patterns in event structures of serendipity. *Information Research* 16(3): Paper 494. retrieved from informationr.net/ir/16-3/paper494.html.

McCay-Peet, L. and Toms, E.G. (2015). Investigating serendipity: How it unfolds and what may influence it. *Journal of the Association for Information Science and Technology* 66(7), 1463–1476. DOI: 10.1002/asi.23273. 4, 18, 21, 23, 24, 28, 30, 47, 49, 60

McCay-Peet, L., Toms, E.G. and Kelloway, E.K. (2014). Development and assessment of the content validity of a scale to measure how well a digital environment facilitates serendipity. *Information Research* 19(3), paper 630. Available at http://www.informationr.net/ir/19-3/paper630. 9, 29, 60

McCay-Peet, L., Toms, E.G. and Kelloway, E.K. (2015). Examination of relationships among serendipity, the environment, and individual differences. *Information Processing and Management* 51, 391–412. DOI: 10.1016/j.ipm.2015.02.004. 20, 22, 25, 29, 31, 47, 57, 60, 61, 67, 69

Mejova, Y., Bordino, I., Lalmas, M., and Gionis, A. (2013). Searching for interestingness in Wikipedia and Yahoo!: Answers. In *Proceedings of the 22nd International Conference on World Wide Web (WWW '13 Companion)* (pp. 145–146). ACM, New York. DOI: 10.1145/2487788.2487858.

Merton, R. K. and Barber, E. (2004). *The Travels and Adventures of Serendipity: A Study in Sociological Semantics and the Sociology of Science*. Princeton, NJ: Princeton University Press. 1, 2, 3, 4, 5, 12, 20, 23, 30

Method. (n.d.). In Merriam-Webster online. Retrieved August 29, 2016, from http://www.merriam-webster.com/dictionary/method. 30

Million, A.J., O'Hare, S., Lowrance, N., and Erdelez, S. (2013). Opportunistic discovery of information and millennials: An exploratory survey. In Grove, A. (Ed.), *Proceedings of the 76th ASIS&T Annual Meeting: Beyond the Cloud: Rethinking Information Boundaries (ASIST '13)* (Article 98). American Society for Information Science, Silver Springs, MD. 31, 57

Morrison, S. and Gomez, R. (2014). Pushback: Expressions of resistance to the "evertime" of constant online connectivity. *First Monday* 19(8). DOI: 10.5210/fm.v19i8.4902. 16

Murakami, T., Mori, K., and Orihara, R. (2008). Metrics for Evaluating the Serendipity of Recommendation Lists. In K. Satoh, A. Inokuchi, K. Nagao and T. Kawamura (Eds.), *New Frontiers in Artificial Intelligence* (Vol. 4914, pp. 40–46). Berlin/Heidelberg:Springer. DOI: 10.1007/978-3-540-78197-4_5. 57

Napier, N.K. and Hoang Vuong, Q. (2013). Serendipity as a strategic advantage? *Strategic Management in the 21st Century* 1, 175–199. 8

Nielsen, P.M., Paay, J., Pearce, J. and Kjeldskov, J. (2015). Exploring urban events with transitory search on mobiles. In *Proceedings of the 17th International Conference on Human-Computer Interaction with Mobile Devices and Services Adjunct (MobileHCI '15)* (pp. 712–719). ACM, New York. DOI: 10.1145/2786567.2793692. 15, 17

Norman, D. and Draper, S.R. (1986). *User Centered System Design; New Perspectives on Human-Computer Interaction*, Hillsdale, NJ: Erlbaum. 33, 34

Nunes, M., Greenberg, S. Neustaedter, C. (2009). Using physical memorabilia as opportunities to move into collocated digital photo-sharing. *International Journal of Human-Computer Studies* 67, 1087–1111. DOI: 10.1016/j.ijhcs.2009.09.007. 13, 27

Oh, S. and Wildemuth, B.M. (2009). Think-aloud protocols. In B. M. Wildemuth (Ed.), *Applications of Social Research Methods to Questions in Information and Library Science* (pp. 178–188). Westport, CT: Libraries Unlimited. 54

Pallot, M., Alishevskikh, A., Holzmann, T., Krawczyk, P., and Ruland, R. (2014). CONEX: Creating serendipitous connections among Living Labs and Horizon 2020 Challenges. In *Proceedings of the 2014 International Ice Conference on Engineering, Technology and Innovation*. IEEE. DOI: 10.1109/ICE.2014.6871569.

Pariser, E. (2011). *The Filter Bubble: What the Internet is Hiding from You.* New York: Penguin Press. 16, 17, 45

Pease, A. Colton, S., Ramezani, R. Charnley, J. and Reed, K. (2013). A discussion on serendipity in creative systems. In *Proceedings of the Fourth International Conference on Computational Creativity*, 64–71. 7, 8

Pessemier, T. de, Dooms, S., and Martens, L. (2014). Comparison of group recommendation algorithms. *Multimedia Tools and Applications* 72(3), 2497–2541. DOI: 10.1007/s11042-013-1563-0.

Pew Research Center (2015). The evolving role of news on Twitter and Facebook. Retrieved July 27, 2016 from http://www.journalism.org/2015/07/14/the-evolving-role-of-news-on-twitter-and-facebook/.

Pittarello, F. (2004). The time-pillar world: A 3D paradigm for the New Enlarged TV information domain. In L. Ardissono et al. (Eds.), *Personalized Digital Television* (pp. 287–320). Netherlands: Kluwer Academic Publishers. DOI: 10.1007/1-4020-2164-X_11. 15

Quality (n.d.). In Merriam-Webster online. Retrieved August 29, 2016, from http://www.merriam-webster.com/dictionary/quality. 26

Quan-Haase, A. and Martin, K. (2012). Digital humanities: The continuing role of serendipity in historical research. In *Proceedings of the 2012 iConference (iConference '12)*. ACM, New York, pp. 456-458. DOI: 10.1145/2132176.2132246. 13

Quan-Haase, A., Martin, K., and McCay-Peet, L. (2015). Networks of digital humanities scholars: The informational and social uses and gratifications of Twitter. *Big Data and Society* http://journals.sagepub.com/doi/abs/10.1177/2053951715589417. 44

Rädle, R., Weiler, A., Huber, S., Jetter, H.-C., Mansmann, S., Reiterer, H., and Scholl, M.H. (2012). eBook meets tabletop: Using collaborative visualization for search and serendipity in online book repositories. In *Proceedings of the Fifth ACM Workshop on Research Advances in Large Digital Book Repositories and Complementary Media* (BooksOnline '12) (pp. 3–6). ACM, New York. DOI: 10.1145/2390116.2390120. 15, 27

Rahman, A. and Wilson, M.L. (2015). Exploring opportunities to facilitate serendipity in search. In *Proceedings of the 38th International ACM SIGIR Conference on Research and Development in Information Retrieval (SIGIR '15)* (pp. 939–942). ACM, New York. DOI: 10.1145/2766462.2767783. 20, 27, 29, 47, 51

Remer, T.G. (1965). *Serendipity and the Three Princes, from the Peregrinaggio of 557*. Norman, OK: University of Oklahoma Press. 2, 3

Renduchintala, A., Kelliher, A., and Sundaram, H. (2006). Creating serendipitous encounters in a geographically distributed community. In *Proceedings of the 1st ACM International Workshop on Human-centered Multimedia (HCM '06)*. ACM, New York, pp. 45–54. DOI: 10.1145/1178745.1178756. 19, 28, 29

Roberts, R.M. (1989). *Serendipity: Accidental Discoveries in Science*. New York: Wiley. DOI: 10.1002/ange.19901021038. 8

Rose-Stockwell, T. (2016). How we broke democracy: Our technology has changed this election, and is now undermining our ability to empathize with each other. Retrieved from https://medium.com/@tobiasrose/empathy-to-democracy-b7f04ab57eee#.alnx6ynf8. 16

Rubin, V. L., Burkell, J., and Quan-Haase, A. (2011). Facets of serendipity in everyday chance encounters: A grounded theory approach to blog analysis. *Information Research* 16(3). Retrieved from http://InformationR.net/ir/16-3/paper488.html. 21, 23, 24, 25, 53, 54

Ruxanda, M.M., Nanopoulos, A., and Jensen, C.S. (2010). Flexible fusion of relevance and importance in music ranking. *Journal of New Music Research* 39(1), 35–45, DOI: 10.1080/09298210903325592. 15

Said, A., Jain, B.J., Lommatzsch, A., and Albayrak, S. (2012). Correlating perception-oriented aspects in user-centric recommender system evaluation. In *Proceedings of the 4th Information Interaction in Context Symposium (IIIX '12)*. ACM, New York, NY, USA, 294-297. DOI: 10.1145/2362724.2362778. 27

Saleem, M., Kamdar, M., Iqbal, A., and Ngomo, A.-C. (2013). Fostering Serendipity through Big Linked Data In: *Semantic Web Challenge*, ISWC2013. 43

Savolainen, R. (2007). Filtering and withdrawing: Strategies for coping with information overload in everyday contexts. *Journal of Information Science* 33(5), 611–621. DOI: 10.1177/0165551506077418. 17

Sawaizumi, S., Katai, O., Kawakami, H., and Shiose, T. (2009). Use of serendipity power for discoveries and inventions. In M. Gen, D. Green, O. Katai, B. McKay, A. Namatame, R. Sarker and B.-T. Zhang (Eds.), *Intelligent and Evolutionary Systems* (Vol. 187, pp. 163–169). Springer Berlin:Heidelberg. DOI: 10.1007/978-3-540-95978-6 11. 51, 52

Schroder, H. M., Driver, M. J., and Streufert, S. 1967. *Human Information Processing—Individuals and Groups Functioning in Complex Social Situations*. New York: Holt, Rinehart, and Winston.

serendipity (n.d.-a). *Dictionary.com* Unabridged. Retrieved from http://www.dictionary.com/browse/serendipity.

serendipity (n.d.-b). *American Heritage Dictionary of the English Language*, Fifth Edition. (2011). Retrieved from http://www.thefreedictionary.com/serendipity.

serendipity (n.d.-c). *Merriam Webster*. Retrieved from https://www.merriam-webster.com/dictionary/serendipity.

serendipity (n.d.-d). *Oxford Dictionaries*. Retrieved from https://en.oxforddictionaries.com/definition/serendipity. 3

serendipity (1932). *Universal Dictionary of the English Language*. New York: E.P. Dutton and Co. 3

Shapiro, G. (1986). *A Skelton in the Darkroom: Stories of Serendipity in Science*. San Francisco: Harper and Row. 6, 40

Shelbe, L. and Wildemuth, B. M. (2009). Research diaries. In B. M. Wildemuth (Ed.), *Applications of Social Research Methods to Questions in Information and Library Science* (pp. 211–221). Westport, CT: Libraries Unlimited. 51

Shneiderman, B., Plaisant, C., Cohen, M., Jacobs, S., and Elmqvist, N. (2016). *Designing the User Interface: Strategies for Effective Human-computer Interaction*. 6th Ed. Pearson. 44

Silverman, R.E. (2013).. The science of serendipity in the workplace: To encourage interaction and innovation, companies try smaller spaces, games; trivia helps break awkward silences. *The Wall Street Journal*. Retrieved from http://www.wsj.com/articles/SB10001424127887323 79810457845508121850870. 13, 14

Solomon, Y. and Bronstein, J. (2016). Serendipity in legal information seeking behavior: Chance encounters of family-law advocates with court rulings. *Aslib Journal of Information Management* 68(1), 112–134. DOI: 10.1108/AJIM-04-2015-0056. 55, 57

Spool, J.M. (2002). The search for seducible moments. UIE. Retrieved from https://articles.uie.com/seducible_moments/. 40

Stewart, K.N. and Basic, J. (2014). Information encountering and management in information literacy instruction of undergraduate, students. *International Journal of Information Management* 34(2), 74–79. DOI: 10.1016/j.ijinfomgt.2013.10.007. 19

Strauss, A. L. and Corbin, J. M. (1998). *Basics of Qualitative Research: Techniques and Procedures for Developing Grounded Theory*. London: Sage Publications.

Sugiyama, K. and Kan, M-Y. (2015). Toward higher relevance and serendipity in scholarly paper recommendation. *SIGWEB Newsletter* winter 2015. DOI: 10.1145/2719943.2719947. 42

Sun, X., Sharples, S., and Makri, S. (2011). A user-centered mobile diary study approach to understanding serendipity in information research. *Information Research* 16 (3). Retrieved from http://InformationR.net/ir/16-3/paper492.html. 18, 21, 23, 24, 25, 51

Swanson, D. and Smalheiser, N.R. (1997). An intractive system for finding complementary literatures: a stimulus to scientific discovery. *Artifical Intelligence* 91(2), 183–203. DOI: 10.1016/S0004-3702(97)00008-8. 42

Swanson, D.R. (1986). Fish oil, Raynaud's Syndrome, and undiscovered public knowledge. *Perspetives in Biology and Medicine* 31, 526–557. DOI: 10.1353/pbm.1988.0009. 42

Taramigkou, M., Apostolou, D., and Mentzas, G. (2017). Supporting creativity through the interactive exploratory search paradigm. *International Journal of Human–Computer Interaction* 33(2), 94–114. DOI: 10.1080/10447318.2016.1220104. 19, 23, 47, 57, 58, 59

Taramigkou, M., Bothos, E., Christidis, K., Apostolou, D., and Mentzas, G. (2013). Escape the bubble: Guided exploration of music preferences for serendipity and novelty. In *Proceedings of the 7th ACM Conference on Recommender Systems (RecSys '13)*. ACM, New York, pp. 335–338. DOI: 10.1145/2507157.2507223. 17

Thudt, A., Hinrichs, U. and Carpendale, S. (2012). The Bohemian bookshelf: supporting serendipitous book discoveries through information visualization. *IN CHI'12*, May 5-10, 2012, Austin, Texas, pp. 1461–1470. DOI: 10.1145/2207676.2208607. 44, 47

Toms, E. G. (1997). Browsing digital information: Examining the 'affordances' in the interaction of user and text. Doctor of Philosophy Thesis, University of Western Ontario, London, ON, Canada. 4, 35, 44, 54, 55, 57, 58

Toms, E. G. (2000a). Serendipitous information retrieval. Paper presented at the *ERCIM Workshop Proceedings*, Zurich, Switzerland. 40, 43

Toms, E. G. (2000b). Understanding and facilitating the browsing of electronic text. *International Journal of Human-Computer Studies* 52(3), 423–452. DOI: 10.1006/ijhc.1999.0345. 36, 41, 47, 61

Toms, E. G. and McCay-Peet, L. (2009). Chance encounters in the digital library. In M. Agosti, J. Borbinha, S. Kapidakis, C. Papatheodorou and G. Tsakonas (Eds.), *Lecture Notes in Computer Science: Research and Advanced Technology for Digital Libraries, 13th European Conference, ECDL 2009*, Corfu, Greece (Vol. 5714, pp. 192–202). Berlin, New York: Springer-Verlag. DOI: 10.1007/978-3-642-04346-8_20. 41, 57

Van Andel, P. (1994). Anatomy of the unsought finding. Serendipity: Origin, history, domains, traditions, appearances, patterns and programmability. *British Journal for the Philosophy of Science* 45(2), 631–648. DOI: 10.1093/bjps/45.2.631. 7, 33, 39, 43, 53

Van den Haak, M. J., de Jong, M. D. T., and Schellens, P. J. (2004). Employing think-aloud protocols and constructive interaction to test the usability of online library catalogues: a methodological comparison. *Interacting with Computers* 16(6), 1153–1170. DOI: 10.1016/j.intcom.2004.07.007. 54

Verhoeven, D. and de Costa V. (2014). HuNI: Helping humanities researchers get lucky [moving image]. Retrieved from http://vimeo.com/bestqualitycrab/huniserendipity. 13

Weeber, M., Klein, H., and de Jong-van den Berg, L. T. W. (2001). Using concepts in literature-based discovery: stimulating Swanson's Raynaud fish-oil and migraine-magnesium examples. *Journal of the American Society for Information Science and Technology* 52(7), 548–555. DOI: 10.1002/asi.1104. 42

Wellman, B. (2004). Connecting communities: On and offline. *Contexts* 3(4), 22–28. DOI: 10.1525/ctx.2004.3.4.22. 12

Whittaker, S., Frohlich, D., and Daly-Jones, O. (1994). Informal workplace communication: What is it like and how might we support it? In *Proceedings of CHI '94*, ACM Press, pp.130–137. DOI: 10.1145/191666.191726. 13

Wildemuth, B. M. (2009a). Direct observation. In B. M. Wildemuth (Ed.), *Applications of Social Research Methods to Questions in Information and Library Science* (pp. 189–198). Westport, CT: Libraries Unlimited.

Wildemuth, B. M. (2009b). Existing documents and artifacts as data. In B. M. Wildemuth (Ed.), *Applications of Social Research Methods to Questions in Information and Library Science* (pp. 158–165). Westport, CT: Libraries Unlimited. 53

William. (2015). The fear of missing out. Retrieved from http://dailypossible.com/the-fear-of-missing-out/.

Williamson, K. (1998). Discovered by chance: The role of incidental information acquisition in an ecological model of information use. *Library and Information Science Research* 20(1), 23–40. DOI: 10.1016/S0740-8188(98)90004-4. 21, 51, 52

Wohlsen, M. (2013). Marissa Mayer's no-working-from-home rule is stupid—or it could save Yahoo. Wired. Retrieved from https://www.wired.com/2013/02/yahoo-no-work-from-home/. 13

Yadamsuren, B. (2013). Potential of inducing serendipitous news discovery in social gaming environment. In *Proceedings of the Annual Meeting of the ASIS&T,* 50, 1–4. DOI: 10.1002/meet.14505001157. 31

Yadamsuren, B. and Erdelez, S. (2010). Incidental exposure to online news. In *Proceedings of the 73rd ASIS&T Annual Meeting on Navigating Streams in an Information Ecosystem*, Pittsburgh, Vol. 47, Article 22. American Society for Information Science, Silver Springs, MD. DOI: 10.1002/meet.14504701237. 23, 30, 31, 55, 57

Yadamsuren, B. and Erdelez, S. (2016). Incidental exposure to online news. In G. Marchionini (Ed.), *Synthesis Lectures on Information Concepts, Retrieval, and Services*. Morgan and Claypool Publishers. DOI: 10.2200/S00744ED1V01Y201611ICR054. 23, 57

Yadamsuren, B. and Heinström, J. (2011). Emotional reactions to incidental exposure to online news. *Information Research* 16(3), paper 486. Retrieved from http://InformationR.net/ir/16-3/paper486.html%5D. 14, 18

Yetisgen-Yildiz, M. (2006). Using statistical and knowledge-based approaches for literature-based discovery. *Journal of Biomedical Informatics* 39(6), 600–611. 42

Zetter, K. (2011). TED2011: Junk food algorithms and the world they feed us. *WIRED* https://www.wired.com/2011/03/eli-pariser-at-ted/. 45

Zhang, Y.C., Ó Séaghdha, D., Quercia, D., and Jambor, T. (2012). Auralist: Introducing serendipity into music recommendation. In *Proceedings of the Fifth ACM International Conference on Web Search and Data Mining (WSDM '12)*. ACM, New York, pp. 13–22. DOI: 10.1145/2124295.2124300. 17, 19, 28, 29, 41

Ziegler, C.-N., Hornung, T., Przyjaciel-Zablocki, M., Gauß, S., and Lausen, G. (2014). Music recommenders based on hybrid techniques and serendipity. *Web Intelligence and Agent Systems: An International Journal*, 12, pp. 235–248. 28

Ziegler, C-N., McNee, S., Konstan, J. A., and Lausen, G. (2005). Improving recommendation lists through topic diversification. In *Proceedings of the 14th International Conference on World Wid Web (WWW'05)*. ACM, pp. 22–32. DOI: 10.1145/1060745.1060754. 41

Zuckerman, E. (2011). Desperately seeking serendipity. Keynote presented at *CHI 2011*, Vancouver, BC, Canada, May 7–12, 2011. Retrieved September 17, 2012, from http://www.ethanzuckerman.com/blog/2011/05/12/chi-keynote-desperatelyseeking-serendipity/. 17

Author Biographies

Lori McCay-Peet works in government in the area of corporate information management and is an Adjunct Professor in the School of Information Management at Dalhousie University in Halifax, Nova Scotia, Canada. Her research focuses on people's perceptions and uses of digital information environments, particularly in the context of knowledge work. Her Ph.D. research, funded by a SSHRC Joseph-Armand Bombardier Doctoral Scholarship, investigated the facets of a digital environment that may facilitate serendipity. She has published and presented her research in several information science and computer science publications and venues including the *Journal of the Association of Information Science and Technology, Information Research, Information Processing and Management*, and the *SIGCHI Conference on Human Factors in Computing Systems*.

Elaine Toms is Professor of Information Innovation & Management in the Management School, University of Sheffield, Sheffield, UK. Prior to this she held posts at the University of Toronto and Dalhousie University (including a Canada Research Chair) in Canada. She researches information interaction in complex information use environments, focusing on the human use of technology to support human tasks and how to evaluate the technology and the processes. Serendipity has been a lifelong research interest from the Ph.D. research when her research design "caused" serendipity to occur, to the present which is now immersed in how we might nurture serendipity in our digital spaces. Along the way her work was supported by a number of research agencies including in particular the Social Sciences and Humanities Research Council of Canada, the Canada Research Chairs Program, and the Canada Foundation for Innovation.

Printed in the United States
by Baker & Taylor Publisher Services